REFLECTIONS FROM THE FLO CROSSROADS

D1595362

MARK TAYLOR

For: Nona
My first book. Sixty-one
true stories

Thanks! Enjoy!

mark Taylor
3/2/99

WHEELOCK CREEK PUBLISHING COMPANY

Printed in the United States of America

Publisher's Cataloging in Publication
(Prepared by Quality Books Inc.)

Taylor, Mark, 1923-
    Reflections from the Flo crossroads/Mark Taylor.
    p. cm.
    Preassigned LCCN: 94-060007.
    ISBN 0-9640038-0-5

        1. Leon County(Tex.)--History. 2. Leon County (Tex.)--Social
life and customs. I. Title

F392.L46T39 1994   976.4'233
                                    QBI94-91

LCCN: 94-060007
ISBN: 0-9640038-0-5

Cover design by Bobbi Shupe, E.P. Puffin & Company
Cover: The Flo Crossroads

First Edition, 1994
10 9 8 7 6 5 4 3 2 1

TO

MY WIFE, RUTH,

AND

MY GRANDSON, ERIC GAY

ACKNOWLEDGEMENTS

First of all I thank my wife, Ruth, for her year long encouragement and support in my research efforts and in the writing of this book. There had to have been many times when she felt my priorities were confused. I also acknowledge the help and moral support I received from Evan and Opal Moore, Billie (Spence) Cooper, and Colonel and Lois Moore in that each provided me with several stories that appear herein. Others that contributed stories and encouragement were Lorene Hood, Wendel Bell, James O. Hill, Kay Moore, Wilson Bell, Miller Lee, Joe Bell and my mother, Winnie Taylor. I also thank those that provided me stories but requested that I not divulge their identities.

I also thank my publishing consultant, Ben McDonald of Word Services, Lakewood, Colorado for his editorial efforts, advice, guidance, and technical assistance in the production of this book.

Bobbi Shupe, of E.P. Puffin & Company, Denver, Colorado deserves my thanks for designing the book cover.

Finally, I must say that the land of my youth, Leon County, Texas and specifically the Flo community and surrounding areas, played a large part in the inspiration for and the production of this book.

INTRODUCTION

There are thousands of rural crossroads in the Continental United States.

Many of these crossroads contain no buildings or have habitation of any kind. Other crossroads may have a house or two, and perhaps even a country store and a church. Anything larger than this would constitute at least a village and I am not addressing any place here large enough to be called a village.

Most country crossroads, whether inhabited or not, have a name. No one knows the name or cares about the name except the local people that live in the area or have lived in the area in the past.

Without exception, every crossroads has a history. Except in very rare cases no one knows the history, or has even heard the history, except those people who were born and raised in the vicinity.

The history of every crossroads is full of strange, humorous, violent, adventurous, and sad incidents that can be of great interest to someone that hears them or reads about them for the first time. Someone may have been born in the crossroads intersection or perhaps died there watching his own blood soak into the dirt by the side of the road.

This book is about a single crossroads out of the thousands, each with its own history, that has a story to tell. I was born near this crossroads and spent the first seventeen years of my life there.

Flo, Texas, located in Leon County, is neither a city, town, nor village. It consists of two country roads that cross each other at right angles. The road through Flo from east to west is a two-lane, blacktop, farm-to-market road while the road from north to south is a dirt road north of Flo and a two-lane, blacktop road south of Flo.

The Flo crossroads has a primitive country store on one corner and a less primitive community church on the opposite corner. No one lives at the Flo crossroads. There is no post office there now, although one existed there some ninety years ago. The place was named after the postmaster's dog, Flo, before the turn of the century. Some two hundred Texans presently live in the Flo community which is identified as the area within five miles of the Flo crossroads.

I was born in the Flo community, one mile west of the crossroads, seventy years ago. I am lucky to have survived my youth there. A significant portion of the population born there before about 1930 failed to make it for various reasons, primarily because of poverty and the lack of medical care and facilities.

This book is about Leon County generally and the Flo area specifically, and is more concerned with the people that live there now, and others that have lived there in the past, than about the geography of the area.

The stories are broken into four groups which cover the years from 1860 through the spring of 1993, or 133 years. The first group of stories is entitled I-POTPOURRI and consists of eleven short, true stories (anecdotes) which will quickly introduce the reader to the overall nature and content of the book. the remaining sections are entitled II - THE EARLY YEARS (1860-1920), III - THE MIDDLE YEARS (1921-1940), and IV - THE LATER YEARS (1941-1993), and consist of fifty more true stories that cover the years indicated in each section title.

All sixty-one stories are true although some have been embellished somewhat at times to clarify them and perhaps make them a bit more interesting. The stories generally fall into the categories of humor, adventure, and human interest (sometimes pathos).

About half of the stories came from my memories of my youth in the Flo community in the 1920's and 1930's. Most of the remaining stories came from the memories of some of the "old heads" that still live there. Some of the stories have come down through the generations from before the turn of the century. A few of the stories are contemporary, covering the period from 1985 through the spring of 1993.

This book might be considered an anecdotal history of Leon County in general and of the Flo area in particular. I have made no attempt to, nor do I plan to, spend the rest of my life searching through old records trying to verify all the statements made in the sixty-one stories. First of all, I am too old (seventy) and I have plans to write many more stories before I hang up my pen (word processor) and paper.

I hope you enjoy reading the book.

Mark Taylor
January 15, 1994
Littleton, Colorado

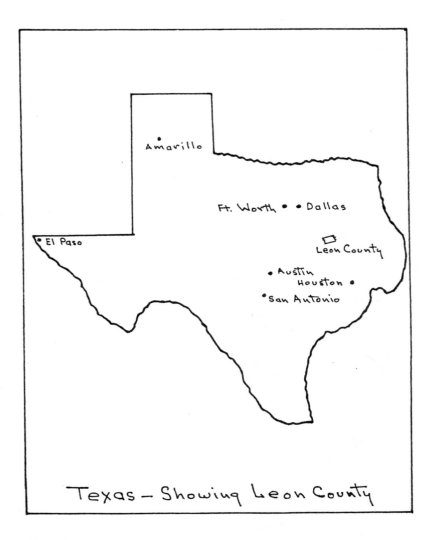

Texas — Showing Leon County

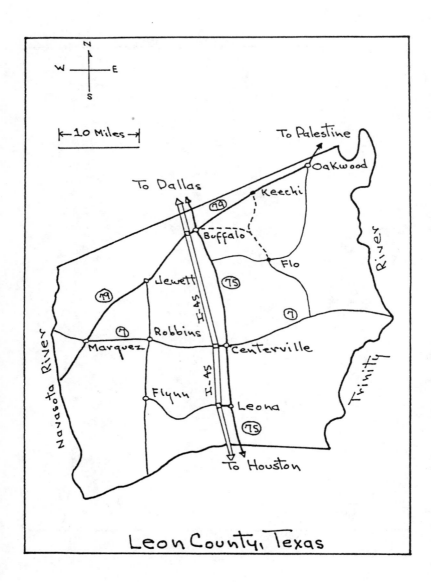

Leon County, Texas

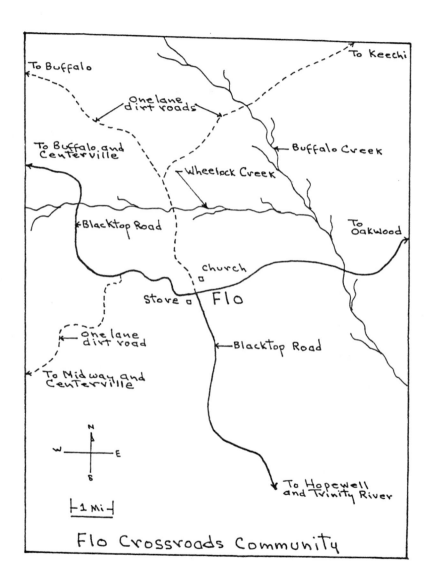

To Buffalo

To Keechi

One lane
dirt roads

Buffalo Creek

To Buffalo and
Centerville

Wheelock Creek

Blacktop Road

To
Oakwood

Church

Store   Flo

One lane
dirt road

Blacktop Road

To Midway and
Centerville

N
W   E
S

1 Mi

To Hopewell
and Trinity River

Flo Crossroads Community

CONTENTS

I - POTPOURRI

HEAVEN IS GOING TO THE FLO STORE

Back in the nineteen-thirties, life in the country crossroads community of Flo, Texas was not so easy as it is now. Every farmer was tired, worn out, and getting old before his time. Going to the Flo store and sitting on the bench in front of it and talking to other farmers from the area was considered a pleasure and a blessing. When not just sitting and talking, one could whittle a lot. Sometimes whittling took place on the very bench on which one sat.

The whittling on the bench got so bad that the front edge of the bench became ragged and uneven. One day Roy Williams, the operator of the Flo store at that time, got his son Gilbert to drive about a thousand nails into the front edge of the bench, about one-fourth inch apart, so that the whittlers wouldn't destroy the bench completely.

While some were whittling, other men and boys would be pitching washers. They used metal washers about three inches in diameter. They pitched the washers at holes in the hard-packed ground which were just slightly larger than the washers. They couldn't afford new horseshoes and had no old, worn out horseshoes because no one in Flo shod their horses.

It finally got to the point where all the men in the area would drop whatever they were doing at the slightest opportunity and go to Flo to sit around the store and spend the day with the other men. If a rain shower came along everyone would quit work in the fields and go to the store. Finally, it got so bad that if a small cloud the size of a handkerchief appeared in the sky that had the slightest possibility of growing into a larger cloud from which rain might fall, they would quit work and go to the store. Any excuse was sufficient. For example, if a strange car drove through the community, within an hour as many as fifty men and boys would be at the Flo store to spend the rest of the day speculating about whose car it could have been, who was driving it, where he was going, and why.

The local preacher was Brother Enoch Parrish, a true believer, who was forever exhorting the men of the community to come to his church, listen to the Gospel as he preached it, and change their sinful ways. His greatest desire was to get the men to spend less time sitting around the Flo store and more time in his church, located directly across the road from the store.

One day Brother Enoch was talking to one of the local men, Uncle Bob Hale, and was pleading for him to come to his church and to bring all the men who wasted their time at the store. His idea was to help them save their souls and to get them into heaven after their deaths.

"Well, Brother Enoch, you see it's like this. None of these men want to go to heaven after they die."

"Where do they hope to go after they die?" asked an astonished Brother Enoch.

"They all hope to go to the Flo store," replied Uncle Bob.

THE BROKEN THERMOMETER

One thing that almost every family in Flo owned during the depression years was a thermometer to determine if an ailing family member had a fever and, if so, to determine their temperature.

Someone in our family broke our thermometer and the old man bought a new one in Buffalo, the nearest town, the next time he went there. When he came home he got all of us together, my mother, sister, two brothers and I and declared that he was going to teach us all how to properly "shake down" a thermometer. One shakes down a thermometer by holding it firmly in his fingers and flicking it downward and then suddenly stopping its downward movement. This forces the column of mercury down in the glass tube so it won't be influenced by the previous reading.

The old man insisted that we watch his action carefully. When he was positive that all eyes were upon him, he flicked the thermometer downward and promptly broke it on the top of a straight-backed wooden chair sitting to his side.

No laughter was heard. Not a smile was seen. The silence was extremely loud as the old man turned red and coughed, stuttered, and made other funny noises for quite some time. Although no laughter was heard or smiles were seen that day in the old man's presence, all of his family members have been laughing about it ever since.

THE MOCKING LAUGH

We had a rural mail carrier for about thirty years named Haney Glenn. Like other mail carriers from the old days, he would assist some of his country customers by doing things like shopping for them in town and delivering their goods to them the next day while delivering their mail. When I was young I was uneasy around him for some reason and avoided him as if he had the plague.

When I was eighteen years old, I decided that I would join the military for service in World War II. By signing up in the fall of 1942 as a "selective volunteer," I was allowed to pick the branch of service I wanted to serve in. I picked the Navy. I was told to go home and wait a few days for my orders to report for induction.

I was anxious to get into the Navy, so I went home and waited for my orders as instructed. I waited near the mailbox, but not *too* near, every day for the next few days when Haney came by delivering the mail. He never spoke a word to me and I certainly did not speak to him. The tension between us was unmistakable.

On the day my orders arrived I was standing about ten feet from the mailbox. To my great surprise Haney got out of his car, came over to me, bowed, handed me my induction papers, and *laughed*! It was the most mocking laugh I have ever heard in my entire life and it left me absolutely speechless. I didn't recover for ten minutes after he left. I felt as if he thought I was trying to dodge the draft and was taking great delight in seeing me nailed by my draft board, when in fact I had volunteered to go into the service.

Haney has been dead for years now. I sincerely hope that, wherever he is, he will not be forced to listen to that same mocking laugh throughout eternity.

4

THE TATTLETALE

Jack Bell's wife died when their daughter, Tommie, was only thirteen years old. Tommie had several older brothers and had two younger brothers, Buddy (five years old) and Woodrow (eighteen months old) that she had to take care of after their mother died. To say that Tommie had her work cut out for her for the following fifteen years or so would be an understatement.

One of my aunts, Bess Pate, was about Tommie's age and she would go visit with Tommie from time to time on weekends when Jack was away from home. The girls would do what they could to entertain themselves and have a little fun while still saddled with the responsibility of taking care of Buddy and Woodrow as well as keeping house, washing clothes and cooking for Tommie's brothers. Their nemesis was one particular older brother, a teen-ager named Joe, who teased them constantly. Even worse, he was a "tattletale" who would tell their father every detrimental thing the girls had done while he was away for the weekend. Jack would then give Tommie a bad time over it.

One weekend Tommie and Bess somehow managed to subdue Joe and tie him to a bedstead because of some tales he had told Jack the previous weekend. They kept Joe tied up for hours and would not release him until he promised to keep his mouth shut about them, including the fact they had tied him to the bedstead. They also told him, in no uncertain terms, that if he did not keep his promise, the following weekend they would tie him up again and beat him with his belt.

Whether Joe was really intimidated by the girls, we may never know. Nevertheless, he stopped telling tales to Jack about Tommie and Bess.

THE YOUNG GAMBLERS

Marquis Taylor and Joe Bell were the same age and friends all their lives. When they were young they were rough, tough, and as uneducated as the other boys their age that lived in the Flo area. They were always into some scheme or another, either to make some easy money, have fun, fight someone, or make love to all the Flo girls.

At fifteen they pooled their money (maybe five dollars each) and went to a cigar-smoking black man that Joe knew and asked him to gamble with their money with the other Negroes. Joe knew this black man was a good gambler. They offered to split the winnings with him. A couple of weeks later the black man handed them fifty dollars each. They both endorsed the fine sport of gambling (shooting craps) on the spot. They spent all the money within a week entertaining a couple of the Flo girls.

In 1993 Joe showed me an old, faded photograph of the black man with the cigar in his mouth. Standing next to him were two hillbilly type teen-age boys with their hands full of money.

Joe and Marquis went to all the country dances in the Flo area when they were young. Dancing and fighting (either right on the dance floor or outside in the yard) were the name of the game. Joe still complains, at age eighty-three, about how he always wound up in the dirt in the yard fighting for his life while Marquis was picking up the very prettiest girl, and sometimes more than one, at the dance.

Marquis and Joe were my boyhood heroes. Marquis died years ago. Joe and I still miss him. When I go back to Texas and visit with Joe, we go to Marquis' grave and talk about the old days.

THE LAS VEGAS SMILE

Shortly after I came back from the Navy on leave in 1945, I happened to stop one day at the local high school, called Lone Star, where my youngest brother, Ralph Kelly, went to school.

Some of the boys were playing around in the schoolyard with boxing gloves. I had sparred a little in the Navy and my brother knew it. Before I knew what was happening, this punk brother had the gloves on my hands. Another kid there named George Smith, who was about my size and weight, but was about four years younger than I, put on the other gloves.

Right then and there I should have remembered and suspected something. What I should have remembered was the Smiths were all fighters and tough as boots. When they fought they came at you with everything they had, as long as they had it, and weren't at all satisfied until you were flat on your back, bleeding profusely. The boys in this family had never heard of the words "spar around a little," which to me meant approach each other, hit a lick or two, then back off and smile and talk a little before approaching each other again.

I remember hearing someone say "Go" and I started to raise my hands to touch gloves in a gentlemanly manner. The Smith boy hit me hard at least nineteen times, within about five seconds, from every conceivable angle. He came at me as if he was trying to kill me. He wasn't satisfied with that so he hit me at least nineteen more times in the same manner. His gloves were coming into my face so hard and fast that I couldn't even breathe much less try to hit him back.

Someone in the crowd of boys said something and suddenly George stopped hitting me and stepped back, presumably to see me fall on my face. Then another boy said something else (I couldn't hear well at all. My ears were ringing from the blows I had just received) and the boxing exercise for George was over. I could have kissed the boy who stopped my punishment, whoever he was and whatever he said.

When I finally got my eyes uncrossed, I looked over at my brother and saw that he was smiling like he had hit the biggest jackpot in Las Vegas. He was not smiling because he had won money on the so-called boxing match. It was simply a sibling rivalry smile, the sort of thing that young Flo boys took very seriously back in those days.

Years later, I thought it had all been forgotten but one day one of my scoundrel brother's sons, my nephew, Gary, casually asked me if I had ever put on boxing gloves with a fellow named George Smith. He was wearing the same smile his father had worn years before on the schoolyard at Flo.

SOME DIED YOUNG

In a place like Flo, Texas the memories and stories of sad and tragic incidents go on and on down through the years. The facts may become somewhat blurred after about seventy-five years or so, but the stories are still repeated at times in hushed tones and with sad countenances.

One incident that is still talked about, at which I was present, occurred near the end of July in 1932. I remember it well for I was at the impressionable age of nine years and was emotionally upset by what happened.

We were at church at the Flo crossroads one Sunday morning. The church was located directly across the dirt road from the Flo store, which at that time was operated by a man named Roy Williams.

During the sermon at the church my first cousin, a boy named Sherill Wayne Hill, who had just turned two years of age, went with his grandfather across the road from the church to the store. Several men and boys were in the store. The store was very primitive and all kinds of merchandise was scattered about, including on the floor. Sherill Wayne found a piece of candy lying on the floor, or perhaps on a shelf in a side area of the store, and broke it into two pieces. He gave one of the pieces to another small boy that was there. This boy dropped his candy either on the floor of the store or outside in the dirt. In any event he abandoned his piece of candy. The good Lord must have been watching over this small boy that day.

Sherill Wayne ate at least part of his piece of candy and immediately became violently ill. The candy had been laced with strychnine to kill rats and mice.

Word spread quickly and the church services broke up immediately as everyone rushed across the road to the vicinity of the store. In my dreams I still hear the wailing of my Aunt Frankie as she ran across the road to her dying son.

There just happened to be a doctor at the church services that morning, a Doctor Brown from Keechi, a few miles north of Flo. He was a country doctor with the limited skills of his profession back in 1932. He may very well not have had his doctor's "pill bag" with him that day. I don't know exactly what he did, if anything, trying to save Sherill Wayne's life but it was hopeless. The boy died about forty minutes after he ate the candy.

No sheriff or lawyer was called. No trip to another doctor or hospital was attempted. No inquest was held. No long term blame was placed upon Roy Williams for poisoning the candy for it was a common thing to do. The entire incident was accepted and considered to be just another product of the times.

In 1992 I went to Brushy Cemetery located a few miles west of Flo. Members of the Hill family are normally buried there. I searched for and found a small tombstone engraved as follows:

SHERILL WAYNE HILL
June 3, 1930 - July 31, 1932

THE CARPENTER

J. B. Pate built houses around Flo for years. He either built or helped build most of the older homes in Flo. He was not the greatest of carpenters, but he was good enough to build the types of houses that were wanted and needed in Flo.

One day a young, newly married friend of his came to him and asked what he would charge to build a small, simple house; more of a shack than a fine home. J. B., knowing that this friend could not afford the materials it would take to build this shack of a house, much less pay for his labor, refused to build it for him and told him to build it himself.

"But I'm not a carpenter," said his friend. "I wouldn't even know how to start building a house."

"Nothing to it," said J. B., "I'll tell you here and now how to get all the advice you'll ever need on how to build your house."

"Tell me," said his friend.

"Go to Buffalo this afternoon and buy yourself a hammer, a saw and a square. On Sunday morning, after all the men in Flo have gathered at the store to do their whittling, spitting and talking, take your new tools and walk slowly past the store. Every damned last one of them will follow you around for the rest of the day telling you exactly how to build your house."

ED'S FIRST AIRPLANE

Ed Lummus had to be a relative of mine. Most of the members of Flo community families, those families that have lived in Flo for the last hundred years or so, are related, in some way. My grandmother was a Lummus and that, of course, makes my being related to Ed a near perfect cinch.

In 1922 Ed was a teen-ager and he ran around with other boys his own age. When they weren't chasing the local girls, the boys were in the woods looking for things like squirrels, swimming holes, moonshine stills and just horsing around as only teen-age boys can horse around. The woods was their sanctuary and they felt more comfortable there than in their own homes, which represented the only civilization (such as it was) that they had ever known.

One day three or four of these boys were down near Buffalo Creek doing whatever was on the agenda for that day, when they heard a strange noise coming at them from across the bottomlands. What they heard was an airplane, but they had never seen nor heard one before. It was making a terrifying sound which scared the boys half to death.

There was an old abandoned house nearby that had once belonged to the Crim family. It had been built in the German manner; that is, it was built above the ground on posts or poles. It was about seven feet above the ground which allowed the livestock to use the area beneath to get out of the weather. The boys raced for the house and clamored their way up the rickety stairs and entered it.

Airplanes in the nineteen-twenties were all slow, loud, and flew at low altitudes. This one was no different, and it kept right on coming, seemingly right at the house. As it got louder and louder the boys looked at each other, wide-eyed, with their hats and caps being slowly raised from their heads as their hair stood on end.

The noise from the airplane got so loud it shook the entire house, or so it seemed to the boys. "It's gonna hit us!" yelled one of the boys. Ed could take it no longer. He jumped to his feet, got a running start across the room, and crashed through the window in the side of the house. The other boys swore that as he was falling the seven feet or so toward the ground he was looking upward to locate this demon that was about to devour them all. He hit the ground running and disappeared into the brush.

Ed lived another seventy years after this incident but he never once took a ride on an airplane. He always took the train instead.

THE GRAPEVINE BOOBY TRAP

In the early nineteen-forties, when the Taylor boys were young they were interested in a family that lived up in the sandflat country near Midway, about five miles from their home in Flo. The reason for their interest in this family was that it contained several rather nice looking girls about the same age as the boys.

From time to time one or another of the boys would be seen dancing with one of the girls at a local country dance. The boys usually rode horses to and from the dances because their father, O K Taylor, would not allow them to use his 1937 Chevrolet pickup truck. The girls also rode horses to the dances when they had no boyfriend who had an automobile, or if his automobile was broken down. If both the boys and girls were on horseback, the boys would somehow manage to ride along with the girls to their home in the sandflat country before returning to their home in Flo.

One moonlit night one of the Taylor boys happened to be riding along with one of the girls on her way home after a dance. They rode side by side down the road, one horse in each rut of the dirt road that meandered across the sandflats. The boy wanted desperately to impress the girl but it was hard to do so on different horses separated by the width of an automobile. They slowly rode and talked about routine things, but all the time the boy was anxiously trying to think of a way to impress the girl.

All of a sudden he had it! He remembered that up ahead, hanging from a tree that grew beside the road, was a grapevine that hung down in a loop from the tree over one of the ruts in the road. The grapevine loop was high enough that he could barely reach it by standing up in his stirrups. The vine was large and strong, about the size of a man's upper arm. He figured it would easily support his weight, so then and there he concocted his plan to thoroughly impress the girl.

When they were about fifty yards from the grapevine he suddenly spurred his horse into a dead run heading straight for the vine. The girl spurred her horse into a run also so that she could stay up with him. As he passed under the loop formed by the vine, doing about twenty-five miles an hour, this brave Taylor lad stood up in his stirrups, dropped his reins on the horse's neck, and grabbed the bottom of the overhanging loop. He expected to swing high in the air as the horse left him, then swing gently to and fro before he finally stopped. Then, he would drop to the ground with a flourish, smiling bravely all the while.

In the middle of his first swing he noted with horror that he was not swinging upward but was more or less going along with the horse, which could only mean that the grapevine was slipping out of the tree instead of lifting him from the saddle. He suddenly found himself about eight feet in the air, his body parallel to the ground, falling rapidly, the horse long gone.

He hit the ground with a solid thud, flat on his back, the wind knocked out of him, the grapevine still in his hands. The only thing that saved him from a worse fate was the fact that the sand upon which he fell was soft.

The girl reined in her mount and came galloping back to his aid, or so he thought.

"Are you all right?" she asked, concern in her voice.

He lay there gasping for breath for a while. She waited. She likes me, he thought. Maybe she'll get off her horse, hold my head in her lap and comfort me. If she does, I'm going to try to kiss her.

"Are you all right?" she asked again. She obviously wanted an answer.

"I think so," he barely managed to croak.

At that precise instant he heard the most ungodly laughter coming from the lips of this fair young maiden, then saw her whip her horse into a run and disappear up the road toward her home.

He lay there for a while longer before finally struggling to his feet. He looked up at the grapevine, which had by now returned to its original position in the tree after he had released it.

"Damn booby trap," he muttered aloud to the vine before limping toward home following the tracks of his horse.

NEVER TRUST A MUSTANG

"When I was about thirteen years old," Wilson Bell, a Flo native said to me, "I was sometimes given the job of going to the Flo store to pick up our meager groceries. This was back in the late nineteen-thirties when many of Flo's residents were near starvation. There was no transportation to go to Buffalo to get groceries and we had to depend on the Flo store to keep us alive, sometimes on credit. I would take a tow sack and walk to Flo, about a mile away, to do our shopping."

"One day I picked up our groceries, which I remember contained, among other things, a twenty-pound sack of flour and a gallon bucket of ribbon-cane syrup. I put them in my tow sack and walked outside to head for home. My older brother, Boyce, had just ridden up to the store on a little mustang pony. I asked him to give me a ride home on the pony and he agreed.

"The mustang was not all that gentle and we had some difficulty getting aboard it, with me and my sack of groceries behind Boyce. We were also riding bareback, meaning our seats were not very comfortable or secure.

"Just as we started to leave Flo, Evan Woodard, a local kid about my age slapped the mustang on the rump and yelled something like, 'What a fine looking horse.' That did it! The crazy horse took off for home at a dead run, with Boyce grabbing for its mane and me grabbing for Boyce. I had Boyce around the waist with my left arm and was trying to hold the sack of groceries out to the side with my right arm.

"Pretty soon we lost it, both of us going head over heels off the pony. We hit the ground so hard that I lost consciousness for a moment. The last thing that I saw was a white cloud engulfing us both. The flour, I thought, I've busted the sack of flour! The first sensation I had when I regained my senses was that I was tasting something very sweet. A moment later I saw that the entire area around us for several yards was a brilliant white, as if it had suddenly snowed on us. I felt something sticky running across my face and discovered that the gallon can of syrup, with its lid missing, was lying on my chest emptying its contents onto my face.

"To go back to the Flo store and replace the ruined groceries was simply out of the question. We had no money for such foolishness. I remember that we ate cornbread three meals a day, including breakfast, for a solid month. We used jelly on the cornbread to make it only slightly more palatable.

"I still remember how fine the pancakes and biscuits eaten with ribbon-cane syrup tasted after this month long ordeal was over. No one can say they saw me carrying our groceries while riding a mustang ever again."

II - THE EARLY YEARS (1860-1920)

12

THE FLO, TEXAS AREA SLAVES

In the spring of 1993, after I had collected and written all the stories in this book except this one, I backed away and took an overall look to get a better perspective of the stories. I felt I needed one more story about the early days in Leon County. I decided to try to get a story about the slaves in the Flo area during and after the Civil War. No one, of course, even at this unique place called Flo was old enough to have been alive during slavery, but I found a man, Sam McGee, whose father was a boy living in the Flo area during the war and whose grandfather owned several slaves himself.

I interviewed Sam and took along my tape recorder to record his story. He eyed the recorder with trepidation and simply refused to tell the story until I put the recorder out of his sight. He didn't mind me recording his voice and story, he just didn't want to see it grinding away while he talked. I placed something between him and the tape recorder and he began his story.

"I want to make a preliminary statement about slaves in general," Sam said. "My father was here when there were slaves during the Civil War and for many years afterward. Slaves weren't as badly mistreated as most people, especially the Hollywood and television people indicate they were, except in some widely separated places and instances. My father always said that people who didn't have enough sense to take care of their slaves didn't have sense enough to warrant their ownership of them. You know that if you have something very valuable you're going to protect it. Almost every owner wanted to take care of his slaves and not make them mad, unhappy or frustrated, for he wanted their cooperation. Of course, slave owners had to have a way to control them. Look how we control prisoners now by spending billions of dollars to try to rehabilitate them, hold them in custody, feed and otherwise take care of them. So we are all like the slave owner in many respects, who at times had to get rough with an unruly, lazy or running slave. Very few slave owners would abuse a slave for fun or revenge, but only roughed him up to the point that his behavior was corrected.

"When my grandmother was a young girl, before she came to Texas with my grandfather, she was attended by a female slave about her own age called a "maid-in-waiting," who helped her take care of herself; things like fixing her hair, helping her dress, and taking care of her clothes. When she married my grandfather she was allowed to take the slave with her to her new home. My grandfather had four or five slaves of his own not long after his marriage. I don't know how he obtained them. Perhaps he purchased them or they were given to him by my great grandfather who was a wealthy man. My grandfather could foresee that the Civil War was likely to free the slaves, so he sold his slaves before he came to Texas with my grandmother and would have sold the maid-in-waiting except for the objections of my grandmother. This slave stayed on in the family for years, even after she had been freed, until her marriage. I believe that after a few years she returned and spent several more years with my grandmother. The slave had a son and when she got old he came and took her home with him and kept her there until she died.

"When the Flo area slaves were freed, most of them took the last name of their former owners. For example, my grandmother's maid-in-waiting took our family name until she married.

"Most of the slave owners in Leon County came to Texas with their slaves because of an advancing Union Army. There was a white family named Reed that came to the area near Flo for this reason. They settled on a farm and were neighbors of my grandfather and his family, which included my father, who was then a young boy. My father and his family knew the Reed family and his slaves as well as one country family usually knows his neighbors. Mr. Reed, unlike his wife, was not much of a businessman or manager.

"They owned rich ground along Beaver Dam Creek which runs through the Flo area. They had a creek bottom field along the creek, but their house was up on a hill where the breeze could blow the mosquitoes away and it would be cooler. Mrs. Reed stayed at home most of the time and would have some of the slave women helping her. She would listen to the other slaves who might be working in the bottom field. As long as she could hear them yelling, talking, whistling, laughing and singing she knew everything was going smoothly, but when they became quiet she knew something was wrong so she would take off her apron and head for the field where they were working.

"One time she arrived there and found that her husband was with them and he had them out in the edge of the timber at one end of the field where they were supposed to be working. They were all gathered around some tall sweet gum trees that had no limbs growing out of their trunks for twenty or so feet in the air. Some of the slave boys had been arguing about their ability to climb trees. So, Mr. Reed had taken the whole group back into the woods to have a contest to determine which one was the best at climbing a tree. The rest of the slaves were gathered around encouraging the boys. When Mrs. Reed arrived she quickly broke up the party. She did not believe that their slaves should be playing games, with or without her husband, when there was work to be done.

"Another time, when the slaves became very quiet, she went to the field and found them sitting in a circle around her husband, who was telling them one of his many stories. Some of the slaves had heard this same story many times, as they had heard all his stories, and were bored to death with it. When he had called them together on this day, a few of them continued to work, so he demanded that they drop their tools and come and listen to his story because he was their owner, wasn't he? I assume he did this with good nature like I might do my grandchildren if I wanted them to listen to what I had to say. Mrs. Reed broke up the story-telling party, to the relief of some of the older slaves, and put them all back to work.

"Mrs. Reed didn't always interfere with his shenanigans, however; especially if they happened to occur during a time when there wasn't much work to be done. One time he made a rule, with her consent, that at Christmas he would allow the slaves to have a Christmas vacation for the period of time that it took the backlog or backsticks they had cut for the family's living room and kitchen fireplaces to burn completely away. A backlog or backstick is a large piece of a tree trunk, a short log, that is used in the back of a fireplace, to keep the fire burning continuously, even at night.

"The Reed's slaves soon began to try to figure out a way to make the backlogs last longer so that their Christmas vacation would last as long as possible. During the summer, when they were not working very hard, they would go down to the creek and cut down the largest sweet gum tree they could find and cut from its trunk two large, short logs. They would then roll these logs into the creek and let them soak in the water until Christmas time. They would then drag them out of the creek and put them in the fireplaces to burn. The water content of these logs was so high that they burned very slowly. Although the Reeds found out about the slaves ruse to obtain more vacation time, they did not change the rule just because they had discovered their secret.

"The Reeds had one unique male slave, a good worker, who might work for months with no difficulty, but would eventually run away. They would get a couple of neighbors to come in to help them find and capture him. He would hide out in the brush all day near the Reed's place and at night he would sneak back to the slave's quarters where the other slaves would feed him. They would tell him where and when the slave owners were going to meet that night to plan their search for him the following morning. Other slaves would eavesdrop on these conversations in order to help him. The next morning he would take off in the opposite direction from the search area.

"During warm weather, he would hide out in the woods for weeks, even though much abused by mosquitoes and ticks. In the winter he would hide out in the cold. When he would get tired of this kind of life he would come back to the Reed's place on his own. Of course, they would give him a thrashing over it. This was no serious beating like Hollywood and television would have us all believe, where every black in the entire United States that was hit by a white man was hit with a twenty-foot bull whip, laying his back wide open. In the vast majority of cases it was more like a whipping one might give an unruly and disobedient child to teach him not to repeat the offense.

"One time this particular slave had disappeared and was hiding out in a marsh on Beaver Dam Creek in a black community now called Pleasant Springs. They were hunting him with a couple of dogs that found him in the marsh. He had a weapon of sorts with him, a blade from a broken scythe, with which he held off the dogs. He couldn't run however, because of the dogs, so they managed to catch him. This may have been the only time they captured him. The other times he merely came back when he was ready. He would then make a good hand for up to a year when he got the urge to run again.

"In another case a slave owner, a neighbor of the Reeds, died and his widow began to have trouble with a certain male slave who did not respect her authority and began to disobey her instructions. She wrote a letter to my grandfather asking him to find someone to help her chastise the slave. She told him what day and time she would send her slave to him to pick up some seed corn so that they could capture him. They were prepared when he arrived and sent him into what was then called a corncrib (it would now be called a barn) to get the corn. As soon as he went inside they went in behind him, closing and locking the door.

"My grandfather stacked his corn ten feet high and would remove it for feeding his stock in such a way that the area from which the corn had been removed appeared as a clear space. This space remained clear as the corn was removed and used even though it was stacked ten feet high around the cleared area. When corn was needed on a daily basis my grandfather would enter the corncrib and pull key ears of corn out of the stack causing perhaps a bushel of corn at a time to fall to the cleared space on the floor. The corn that fell was then taken from the corncrib and fed to his stock or was taken to the local gristmill where it was ground into cornmeal.

"When the disobedient slave entered the corncrib and was followed by my grandfather and his neighbor, they all entered into the space with the cleared floor. When the slave realized they were about to manhandle him, he made a run at the ten foot stack of corn that practically surrounded them and tried to climb it to get to the open gabled end of the corncrib. As he was climbing, corn kept falling on him from above as he dislodged the lower ears of corn. The harder he climbed the more corn fell upon him from above. As a result he could not escape and they captured him, tied his hands and thrashed him, but not to the point that blood was drawn. They then let him go and sent him on his way with the bag of seed corn he had come for. From that time on the slave never disobeyed his lady master again, for he had learned she wouldn't tolerate his disobedience.

"I believe the Reed family's slaves either left the Flo area or died out because there have been no blacks in the area by that name in my lifetime. There were perhaps a dozen freed slaves in the area, however, that began to homestead land after they obtained their freedom. Some of these old homesteads that had come down to their black descendants have been sold within the last twenty years, after the price of land became so high, to mostly white people from the Houston area.

"Some descendants of slaves still live in the Pleasant Springs area not far from the Reed family farm. They ran their stock on the open range since the Civil War and had a sentimental attachment to the land. They hated to see it sold, broken up into smaller plots, fenced and otherwise modernized, but they sold much of the land nevertheless. One black descendant, George Hopkins, told me not long ago, 'Them crazy white folks from Houston would pay a big price for a worthless piece of land up a tree!' This may sound a bit odd but the man got his point across only too well.

"There was a freed slave, whose name was Andy Hughes, who was about my father's age when he was freed; that is, ten or twelve years old. He didn't grow up to be a big man, but he was tough and energetic. He made it as best he could. When he married he moved into an abandoned little shack in the Pleasant Springs area. Several different black families had lived in the shack, but would move out after a year or so. The land around the little place didn't have very good timber for even building fences. At least that was the excuse these blacks had used that had abandoned it.

"After a few short years, Andy Hughes had most of the place cleared, fenced, crossfenced, and even had a lane running through the field to his house. He was a good manager and worker all his life. When Andy died in the nineteen-twenties, he owned over seven hundred acres of land, all the good teams he needed, with good harnesses, good wagons, and sound buildings. He had started out with 160 acres of ground and had bought surrounding land. He had a good black stallion saddle horse, and the woods were full of his hogs and cattle. He also had money and he had no problems with anyone, white or black. He had a room in his house that had a bed in it that was reserved for the use of white men that no black man had ever slept in. Traveling white men, including politicians that were running for office, would come by his place and spend the night. When he needed a favor from anyone, black or white, he could get it.

"Several other blacks in the area also did well. John and Lige Campbell's father did well, around 1880, working hard and buying land in the area where they lived. John Chase also did well around 1900. If these men could do well in the days after the Civil War, I find it hard to believe that the freed slaves and their descendants were as downtrodden as Hollywood would have us believe.

"John Campbell had a son that ran around with a white man in the early nineteen-thirties. They were hog thieves. Lee Thompson, the sheriff of Leon County, found enough evidence against the white man to send him to prison but he could never get any hard evidence against the black man. After the white man went to prison, the black stopped stealing white men's hogs and began to steal hogs from other blacks. They didn't own many hogs and those he stole were the hogs they needed for food and lard. The blacks in the area complained to the sheriff and told him exactly who was stealing their hogs. Lee went to him and said he knew he was the thief, although he had no hard evidence against him. He also reminded him that he had sent his white fellow thief to prison. 'You have two choices,' he said, 'you can leave the county and never come back, or I'm going to kill you. Make up your mind and make it up now!'

Campbell left the county that night and did not return until he was an old man.

"That's the end of my story about the slaves in Leon County," said Sam. "I never thought there would come a time when someone would come to me and be interested in it."

"It's an interesting story from the old days," I said to him. "I know the people in Leon County, and especially those in the Flo area will be interested in reading it."

THE LEON COUNTY GUNFIGHTERS

"The story that I am about to tell you," said Jim Story, "cannot possibly be one hundred percent true because it has come down to me from at least a half dozen sources from the old days, which almost guarantees that a certain portion of it is inaccurate. As a matter of fact, there is more than one version of some of the details and I have elected to tell you the version that I believe to be the most logical, believable and hopefully the most truthful. All my sources for this story have passed away, some of them as much as eighty years ago. All were reliable and honest men and I firmly believe that each of them was telling me the truth as he knew it."

Jim looked at me with his watery, pale eyes and waited. I knew he expected me to decide then and there whether or not I should turn on my recorder. He knew I was in pursuit of true stories from the old days about Leon County and its people. He did not know whether or not his story would meet my criteria. I saw the tremor in his ninety year old hands as he awaited my decision.

"Tell me, Jim," I said, "just what percentage of this story do you think I should believe is generally true, not specifically and literally true, but generally true?"

"Eighty-five percent," he said immediately as if he had already given it some careful thought. "Plus or minus a percentage point or two."

"Does this fifteen percent gray area involve major actions that take place in the story?"

"No. Almost all the questionable things involve minor things here and there in the story."

"Okay, Jim. I want to hear the story. Just relax and tell it to me slowly and completely." I turned on the recorder and Jim started his story:

"This story starts about 1865 and covers a period of about twenty-five years. It concerns two families, one named Hardin and the other named Lenson. The men in both families were tough, aggressive, woman chasing, fighting, drinking and gun packing types. I guess the Spanish word for them would be *hombres*.

"About 1865 a man named Hardin lived near the Trinity River in Leon County. He was a strong-willed businessman, a tough customer both from a business and a physical standpoint. He headed a group of his hired hands, who were also rough and tough types, and controlled them with an iron fist. One of his hired hands, who was in charge of other hired hands, began to get out of line and one day he disappeared. Many believed that Hardin killed the man or had some other member of his gang kill him.

"There has been some speculation over the last hundred years that this particular Hardin was a relative of the infamous outlaw and murderer John Wesley Hardin, who was considered the fastest gun in all of Texas back in his heyday. However, there is no evidence that I know of that links the two.

"Thousands of acres of land in Leon County in those days were owned by absentee landowners. Much of this land was along the Trinity River, which forms the eastern border of the county, and was very rich ground, ideal for farming and ranching. This land, as was most other land in the county, was unfenced and therefore was open range land. This meant that the land was available to everyone who wished to run cattle on it.

"Hardin had many cattle and they used this open range land, which he more or less controlled. This did not satisfy him, however, for he wanted to own this land outright. He was a shrewd businessman and he figured out a way to get ownership of some of this land without spending a dollar.

"He forged deeds for portions of the land which showed transfer of these lands to himself by former owners years before. He folded, creased, and wrinkled the deeds for several days and aged them by pouring coffee over them and placing them in the hot sun to weather for a few days.

"When he was ready with the deeds, he had his gang split up into two groups. Some of them rode horseback to the state capitol in Austin, Texas a hundred miles to the west, while the others rode into Centerville, the county seat of Leon County. The two gangs then burned the courthouse in Centerville and the land office in Austin (both were wooden buildings) at the same time, destroying all the land deeds that were stored in both places. This was the night of November 9, 1885.

"The people that owned the land Hardin wanted now were expected to present evidence that they were the legal owners of their land by producing a deed to the property they were trying to reclaim. Most land owners had no such deed, of course, but Hardin did--his manufactured and artificially aged deeds. Hardin, therefore, ended up being the legal owner of most of the land he coveted.

"Hardin had many enemies in Leon County, any one of which might decide to kill him if he got the chance. Therefore, he began to take precautions to protect himself. Knowing that his large wooden ranch house would not provide the necessary protection in case of a gunfight or a fire, he built himself a small rock house with thick walls, perhaps fifty feet or so from his ranch house. He built several small portholes in the sides of this fortress through which guns could be fired. Back in those days, about 1880 I suppose, Leon County people believed that one could not shoot bullets inside a horseshoe at any reasonable distance, so Hardin had horseshoes mounted against the rock walls around the portholes.

"Years later the story came out that he had dug a tunnel underground from his ranch house to the rock fortress through which he and others could crawl if his ranch house were burned to the ground during a gunfight. The tunnel could be closed where it entered the rock fortress to prevent smoke from entering. The tunnel would not be discovered by his enemies until a few days after the ranch house had burned because of the smoldering embers of the ranch house. The discovery could be delayed even longer than that because the ranch house area would be under fire from the rock fortress.

"I saw this rock fortress several times in the nineteen-twenties when I was a young man. The ranch house had disappeared years before but the rock fortress was still standing with its portholes outlined with the horseshoes. Later, the rock fortress disappeared. Someone told me that it had been destroyed by a tornado.

"Back in those days it was common for rural people to move around the country a lot. A typical case would be that a family was moving as they were passing through Leon County on their way across the state. Their belongings might be carried in two or three wagons and they would be herding their livestock along with them. Sometimes the Trinity River would be at flood stage and the family would be held up for a week or two at the river. When the water receded they would ford the river, which usually meant a certain amount of swimming in the river had to occur, or they used a ferry, which was no more than a large raft, with a wire cable anchored on each side of the river. The cable was used to pull the ferry back and forth across the river.

"While the family was waiting to cross the river, Hardin would invite them into his ranch house, be cordial to them, and invite them to stay there until the river subsided. Many times though, the family members would subsequently disappear and all their possessions and livestock, would become Hardin's property.

"Hardin was said to have occasionally hired gangs of Mexicans to build levees along the river at places to protect his farmland from the floodwaters. When the levees were finished, or nearly finished, he would kill or have killed the man that ran the crew and his closest associates and bury them in the levee they had built for him.

"You should understand that I have a difficult time believing all these stories that Hardin would murder a whole family that was staying with him while waiting to cross the river or murder several men who had built a levee for him, even though the men that related the stories to me firmly believed they were telling the truth.

"Over a period of years Hardin kept raising and trading cattle in Leon County and eventually ended up owning a lot of land in the vicinity of Jewett, about

41

thirty-five miles northeast of where he lived near the Trinity River. Jewett may be the oldest town in Leon County. He raised cattle on this land, which was also open range country.

"Other ranchers had cattle on this land and wanted to "cut" Hardin's herd (which means they wanted to ride through his herd from time to time to look for their own stock). This was a practice accepted by almost all ranchers and was a necessary consequence of the open range system of raising cattle. Hardin did not go along with cutting of his herd by other ranchers and he flatly refused to allow it. The only conclusion that the other ranchers could draw from his refusal was that he was stealing their cattle.

"Another rancher, who had several sons, lived near Buffalo about nine miles east of Jewett. This family was also noted for its aggressiveness, toughness, and no-nonsense approach to matters of interest to them. This family's name was Lenson.

"The ranchers in the Jewett area, who were having trouble with Hardin and his men, hired the elder Lenson's oldest son to come to Jewett and cut Hardin's herd. Lenson's son, along with others in his family, had a reputation for being fighters. He wore twin pistols on his hips to back up his reputation and he was respected, as gunmen can be respected, by everyone that knew him, including members of the Hardin gang who had similar reputations.

"Lenson cut himself a persimmon switch about six feet long and rode into Hardin's herd to search for and separate the other Jewett rancher's cattle from Hardin's cattle using the switch to urge them along.

"It is not known whether Lenson found other rancher's cattle in Hardin's herd, but I know that

Hardin's people were mad as hell at him for cutting their herd.

"The Hardin men didn't challenge Lenson or try to stop him in any way. Although they undoubtedly had tough men that also wore pistols they knew that if they decided to stop Lenson there would be a killing. They apparently decided that the time, circumstances and place were not right for a confrontation. This standoff was the beginning of a deadly feud between Hardin and the Lenson family.

"Later, perhaps as early as a month or as long as a couple of years, some of the Jewett ranchers hired the same Lenson, along with a black man he knew and who may have worked for the Lensons, to help them deliver a herd of cattle somewhere west of Jewett.

"On their way back to Buffalo, Lenson and the black man were riding together, having separated from the others sometime earlier. Jewett was not exactly on their straight route to Buffalo, but it was not very far off this path. Lenson decided that he needed a cigarette, but neither he nor the black man had any matches with them. Lenson decided they would ride into Jewett and pick up some matches and perhaps have a drink in one of the saloons. The black man tried to talk him out of it and told him that some of the Hardin men were undoubtedly in town and that he would be outnumbered and might be killed. Lenson ignored his advice.

"They rode into Jewett and stopped in front of one of the saloons. The saloon occupied the ground level floor of a hotel building that was at least two stories high. Lenson went into the saloon to ask for matches and have his drink. The black man, not being allowed in a white man's saloon, stayed outside with the horses. When Lenson entered he saw several of

Hardin's men. He got his matches and his drink and began to enter into a conversation with them. They did some drinking, talked about their differences, ironed them out, called a truce, and shook hands on it. Lenson then went outside to get on his horse and leave.

"As soon as Lenson stepped out the door a lawman, who happened to be in the saloon, immediately deputized two of Hardin's men for the purpose of arresting Lenson. No one seems to know who this lawman was; perhaps he was the sheriff or a deputy sheriff of Leon County. Furthermore, no one knows what charges they were going to bring against Lenson.

"One of the deputized men went upstairs to cover Lenson from a window of the hotel overlooking the street. The other one went outside on the street where Lenson was lighting up a cigarette and told Lenson that he was under arrest. Lenson, being an experienced gunfighter, knew they had set a trap for him and sensed that another of Hardin's men was stationed at the window above him. He promptly went for his guns and killed the man in the window then shot the man on the street but not before the man had also shot him.

"Lenson was not killed instantly but was down on the ground, completely disabled. The black man, who was not armed and had watched it all, loaded Lenson on his horse and left town headed for Buffalo. Lenson died shortly thereafter, perhaps by the time he had left Jewett.

"Now of course the die had been cast, so to speak. It was no longer a simple disagreement between two groups or gangs but was now a full blown blood and guts war between the Hardin gang and the Lensons.

"The elder Lenson, the dead man's father, decided to go after Hardin himself instead of Hardin's gang. He decided that he would take his time about it, however. Although Hardin was not in on the actual firing of the guns that killed his son, the father had no doubt that he had previously advised his men to kill his son if the opportunity to do so presented itself. Over a period of several weeks or months the elder Lenson became very familiar with Hardin's habits, where he operated, how he operated, and most of all he learned about when and where he traveled.

"Late one evening the elder Lenson rode his horse to Flo at a brisk but not punishing pace, left his horse and borrowed another horse from a man that lived about a mile east of the crossroads. This man owned a string of fine horses. I have never learned of what interest this horse owner had, if indeed any, in either the Hardin gang or the Lensons. Perhaps he had a grudge against Hardin or thought he was doing the county a favor by helping get rid of him, or perhaps he owed Lenson a favor. In any event, Lenson headed at a gallop down the road toward the Trinity River on the old dirt road called Kickapoo Shoals Road and finally arrived at an area called "Hardin's Store," about ten miles from Flo. Later, in 1900, after the Hardins had left the area, the name was changed to "Malvern". Some vestiges of Malvern can still be seen along this road today.

"Lenson stationed himself beside the road, hid in the brush, and waited. Soon Hardin himself came along this road on horseback. A storm was in progress and the night was very dark because of the cloud cover. Lenson was essentially blind in the darkness except when lightning flashed every few seconds. When Hardin rode past and Lenson recognized him, he waited for the next lightning flash and shot at Hardin's head with a double-barreled shotgun loaded with buckshot. Just before he pulled the triggers, Hardin's horse stumbled in the dark, having stepped into a depression in the road, going down almost to his knees. This caused the buckshot to go over Hardin's head. Some say that the buckshot actually knocked his hat off.

"Lenson didn't stick around to verify that he had actually killed Hardin. He jumped on his horse and rode at top speed back to Flo where he left him, mounted his own horse and rode at a moderate pace back to Buffalo thinking that he had avenged the death of his son.

"The reason he had ridden the horse so hard between Flo and Hardin's Store, yet leisurely rode his own horse between Flo and Buffalo was to set up an alibi, in case one was needed. If arrested on suspicion of murder he could point to the hour he left and returned to Buffalo and state that no horse was capable of covering around forty miles in about four hours and the fact that his horse was neither winded nor wet with sweat upon his return to Buffalo. He was never accused of attempting to murder Hardin that night.

"Lenson never did manage to kill Hardin nor was he killed by Hardin. It may have been because Lenson didn't live long after he tried to murder Hardin.

"I have heard that the Lenson's trouble-making, drinking and fighting began to have detrimental effects on some of the operating businesses in Buffalo along about this time, one being the Pearlstone General Mercantile store.

"Pearlstone's store was noted throughout Leon County and the surrounding area for being the one place that could sell you anything that you might need. In fact is was noted as a cradle to grave store that could sell diapers and safety pins for babies as well as caskets and tombstones for those that had died from old age. It could also sell you anything you might need in between.

"The Pearlstones were Jewish and they believed in taking care of each other and their business interests. When something was going wrong in one of their enterprises they believed in taking care of the problem sooner rather than later.

"As a result of the problems they were having with the Lensons, they hired a man, a stranger to Leon County named Miller, to be a clerk in their store. There was some speculation that Miller may have been a gunman that had been reported as disappearing from the area around Austin some time earlier. In any event, the clerk began having trouble with one of the Lenson men over a beautiful woman. The woman was a doctor's wife and she was well-to-do. She rode around in a beautiful buggy, I guess one would call it a surrey, pulled by a fine horse. She didn't live in Buffalo but she would visit there from time to time and would buy all kinds of fine things from the Pearlstone store.

"Miller and one of the Lensons got into trouble over this woman. I have heard that it involved a letter from the woman to Miller that, somehow, Lenson had obtained. He was talking about the contents of the letter to others and was showing it around town. The problem became very serious and soon other people in Buffalo began trying to calm both parties to avoid even more serious problems.

"One morning several of the Lensons decided to kill Miller and walked down the street toward Pearlstone's store. Miller saw them coming and opened fire on them. He killed the elder Lenson immediately. It was reported that the store had a good supply of guns for sale and plenty of ammunition and that while Miller was firing at the Lensons another clerk was loading several guns to provide Miller the fire power he needed. Meanwhile, the Lensons had taken what shelter they could find and were firing at the store. The Pearlstone store was made of rock and their bullets were essentially ineffective against it.

"After killing the elder Lenson, Miller killed another of his sons and perhaps wounded another when they left their shelters and went into the street to try to help their father. Finally the Lensons got a wagon and team and drove them down the street, taking shelter behind the wagon, to try to pick up their dead and wounded. Miller could have shot the team but that would not have caused the Lensons to be exposed so the gunfight ended there and the Lensons proceeded to pick up their dead and wounded.

"Miller was arrested and tried for his crime but the Lensons had antagonized so many people in and around Buffalo that many of them came to Miller's aid and he was not convicted. After the trial, a friend of Miller who had helped him avoid conviction went to him and told him that he should leave Leon County and never return because if he stayed there it would only lead to more trouble. Perhaps this man was Miller's lawyer. Miller disagreed with him and told him that he had 'got the Lenson captain.' The friend's reply was that 'all the Lensons are captains.'

"The youngest Lenson, whose first name was Eugene, was not involved in the gunfight or at least was not wounded in the gunfight. He decided to avenge the death of his relatives. He purchased a pair of .22-caliber pistols, mounted on .45-caliber pistol frames and practiced with them constantly. He would daily go to a

48

ravine outside Buffalo and practice drawing and firing the pistols for hours. Eventually he was ready to take on Mr. Miller.

"Miller was known to pass through Jewett on the train regularly. Eugene Lenson made arrangements with someone in Jewett, some say the railroad ticket office clerk, to notify him when Miller passed through Jewett on his way back to Buffalo. One day Lenson got the word that Miller was due to arrive in Buffalo on the train, so he went to the depot armed with a pair of .45-caliber pistols which had replaced the .22-caliber pistols. Another party there, also waiting for Miller, got on the train and warned him that Lenson was waiting to kill him and told him to stay on the train. Miller, who was also wearing a gun, apparently felt he was capable of taking care of himself, so he left the train.

"When the two men met, they went for their guns and Lenson was the faster man, thanks to all the practicing he had done drawing and firing his pistols. He shot Miller down. As he was lying there, slowly dying, someone tried to come to his aid. Lenson ordered them to stay back saying something like, 'Stand back! That son-of-a-bitch made my daddy lay out in the street and die by himself and he's going to do the same thing!'

"Within a few minutes Miller was dead and when the train pulled out Lenson stepped aboard it and rode it into Palestine Texas, about thirty-five miles east of Buffalo. There he turned himself in to the law. He was tried in the courts but was not convicted. He never spent a day in jail after the trial.

"Back in those days most people in Leon County did business with the Pearlstone store on credit. If a man ran up a bill that got too large, the store would stop selling to him until he paid all or at least part of his bill. If the debtor continued to refuse to pay or simply couldn't pay all his bills, the store would turn over the bills to a third party to collect, paying him ten percent of what he could collect.

"One man that Pearlstone turned over their bill collecting duties to, a rather shiftless hanger-on around town, on his first day on the job rode out of Buffalo, heading east. He came to a farmer's place and showed the farmer his bills and told him that Pearlstone had sent him to collect their money. The farmer paid him off then and there. He rode on to the next debtor's place and went through the process again. This man paid him off as well. About noon he arrived at another debtor's place, located in Keechi a few miles east of Buffalo. He found the farmer trying to plow in a raw new-ground field with a balky team of mules in a temperature of about one hundred degrees in the shade and there was no shade. A raw new-ground field is one that has never been plowed before and has just been cleared of brush and timber. There are stumps still sticking up all over it. If you manage to get the plow in the ground at all, you won't plow more than three feet before you hit the roots of one of the recently felled trees at which time you stop with a gut-wrenching jolt.

"This bill collector had by now decided that he would make bill collecting his lifetime job. As a matter of fact he was chastising himself for not having discovered such a profitable job years earlier. He got off his horse and hopped over the farmer's fence just as the farmer arrived at the end of the row near him. This farmer was already mad as hell and was sweating like a pig before the bill collector said his first word. He advised the farmer of why he was there and asked him

50

to pay up immediately. The farmer ripped the plowlines off his shoulders, threw them on the ground and headed for him on the run with balled fists and blazing eyes. The bill collector heard him say, 'I'm going to beat the hell out of you!'

"The bill collector instantly lost all interest in his work and jumped the fence, got on his horse and raced away back toward Buffalo. When he got to Pearlstone's store he barged in, paid them the money he had collected, got his ten percent and said, 'I quit. This ain't no damn job for me!'

"Eugene Lenson got the job of collecting Pearlstone's delinquent bills, perhaps because he had a proven reputation for being tough. One day he took some bills to "Little" Dick Woods, the son of "Big" Dick Woods, and tried to collect on them. Back in those days people didn't use words like "Dick Woods Senior" and "Dick Woods Junior" but would refer to the senior as "Old" or "Big" and to the junior as "Little" or "Young". Little Dick looked over the bills and told Lenson that the bills belonged to his father who had the same name and initials. Lenson went on his way, temporarily satisfied, but for some reason he failed to collect from Big Dick Woods, perhaps because he had moved away or simply couldn't pay them.

"Some time later Lenson, who was drunk at the time, was in a saloon in Oakwood about fifteen miles east of Buffalo, when Little Dick Woods walked in. He immediately confronted Little Dick and demanded payment for the bills. Little Dick again explained the situation and stated that the bills belonged to his father. Lenson became irate and cursed him in front of the crowd and even spat in his face. Little Dick stood there and took it. He would have been foolish to have done otherwise. He soon managed to slip out of the saloon and rode his horse down the street to the local hardware store where guns were for sale. He asked the store owner to sell him a double-barreled shotgun and a box of buckshot loaded shells. The owner wanted to make a sale, but was a little concerned about what Little Dick would do with the shotgun (he had heard what had happened in the saloon). He sold Little Dick the shotgun after getting him to promise that he would head for home with the shotgun immediately after leaving the store. Little Dick agreed to do so.

"Little Dick took the shotgun, loaded both barrels, and tied it to his saddle. He then sat down on the sidewalk in front of the store and thought about it for a while. Then, he got on his horse, rode back to the saloon, removed the shotgun from his saddle, and stepped into the saloon with it.

"The first thing he saw was Eugene Lenson shaking hands with the bartender and heard him tell the bartender about how tough and bad he was. Little Dick called Lenson's name and when he turned toward him shot him with both barrels of the shotgun, killing him instantly. Little Dick was arrested and tried for the murder of Eugene Lenson but was not convicted. Such was the justice of the times.

"When I was a young man, I met Little Dick Woods, who was already an old man by then, and he told me the story about his troubles with Eugene Lenson," said Jim. "He told the story as the gospel truth and I have no reason to disbelieve any part of it."

"That's the end of my story about the Hardins and the Lensons," said Jim. "Do you think you can use it in the book of true stories that you are writing about the old days in Leon County?" He was watching me closely, concern in his eyes.

"That's a tough question to answer right at the moment," I replied, "but I can assure you that if it doesn't end up in this particular book it will most certainly end up in another of my books where the requirements for truthfulness aren't quite so severe."

"I understand that. It's okay," he said but I could see the disappointment in his eyes. I knew he wanted his story to appear in this book because he knew that it would be distributed throughout the county and everyone in Flo and the surrounding communities would have a chance to read it.

"Why don't you research the story I have told you and verify what is true and what is possibly not true? Most of the information must exist somewhere in the old Leon County records, or old copies of county newspapers, or at the state capitol in Austin. For example, it shouldn't be too difficult to verify whether or not the Leon County courthouse and the land office in Austin burned the same night or at least within a few days of each other."

"I know how to do the research, Jim, but you've got to realize that I live in Colorado and that I am already seventy years old and I simply don't have the time to spend an entire year researching your story just to determine its relative truthfulness. My time is running out and I have a great number of stories that I hope to write before I have to hang it up. I hope you understand."

"Peace brother," he said, offering me his hand.

After writing Jim's story and studying it carefully, I finally decided to include it in this book. Although parts of it don't quite measure up to other stories in

53

reliability, I decided to state at the beginning of the story that even Jim himself considers at least fifteen percent of the story to be inaccurate or at least questionable.

14

THE COUNTRY DOCTOR

My grandfather, William F. Taylor, was a doctor who lived in the Flo community from 1895 until his death in 1925. He doctored everyone, within about ten miles of where he lived, that was willing to call upon him. He either rode a horse or used a horse drawn buggy to go to his patient's homes to treat them. In his later years he started riding a jenny (a female donkey), and usually wore one of his daughter's straw hats which had a wide red band and long colorful ribbon streaming down from it. If a patient was seriously ill he would spend several days and nights at the patient's home waiting for him either to get better or die.

Doctor Taylor had no formal training at an accredited medical college but rather got his doctor's certificate at the age of thirty-seven by going before a medical board in Clarksville, Texas in 1893. The medical board interviewed and orally questioned him for two days. He reported to his family years later that the medical questions he was asked weren't too difficult to answer, but his feet hurt him so badly from standing so long that he almost walked out of the interview. At the time he had almost concluded that he didn't want to become a doctor. He also reported that he became interested in medicine because he lost several of his children when they were babies. In his opinion, the babies had died because of bad water and because of flies and mosquitoes.

Doctor Taylor made many of his own medicines. He concocted a solution he called his "Taylor Tonic" or

"Red Tonic," which he dispensed to almost everyone that he called upon. He made his children take a dose of it every morning. He also called a medicine he made for women his "Squawnky Doodle Pills." He also made a cough medicine out of carbolic acid and water that you were expected to gargle to stop a cough. My father made some of this stuff himself years after Dr. Taylor died and we kids were forced to use it. After I grew up I realized that the carbolic acid deadened the throat to some extent, as any acid would be expected to do, and therefore would stop the "tickle" in the throat that caused one to cough. One time Dr. Taylor gave a Negro man a bottle of the cough medicine, but didn't get it across to him how he should use it. The man drank the whole bottle at one time and his friends and family had to walk him all night to keep him from passing out and dying.

Doctor Taylor regularly delivered babies (he delivered me, his grandson), pulled teeth, lanced boils, sewed up wounds, set broken limbs, and treated people for colds, pneumonia, diphtheria, yellow jaundice, malaria (called chills and fevers), scarlet fever and other ills. He was not a surgeon and did no surgery except a few emergency cases. He once operated on a woman named Edna Selman Rich and removed her appendix. He did this on her kitchen table at night using the light from a kerosene lamp. How she lived is a mystery since it is extremely unlikely that the good doctor properly sterilized either himself or his operating tools before performing the surgery.

In another case he operated on a black lady who had breast cancer, removing her breast in the process. She did not survive the surgery for more than a day or two. He once attended a man whose head had been smashed by a bucket of mud that had fallen on him while he was cleaning out a well. He laid the man out on the front porch and spent several hours picking the pieces of shattered skull out of his battered head and exposed brain. He lived for years afterward and was not much worse off because of his ordeal. This man's granddaughter still lives in the Flo area and told me about his accident and Doctor Taylor's help.

Doctor Taylor was a self-educated man and was known for reading, especially his medical books, every night until well past midnight.

One of the strange things Doctor Taylor did was enter the name "Marion" on the birth certificate of at least three of his grandsons (including me), without their parent's knowledge or consent. He apparently loved the name "Marion," and once told one member of his family that his real name was "William Marion Franklin Taylor."

After I grew up I began to realize that when Doctor Taylor died, he owned at least a half dozen farms scattered around the Flo area. These farms were seventy-five to one hundred and sixty acres each and were divided among his children when he died. My father inherited at least two of these farms and they are still in our family. Over the years I have talked to many people in the Flo area who personally knew Doctor Taylor. To my surprise I have never heard anyone say anything detrimental about his business dealings. I had thought, perhaps, that he might have pressured some of his patients to deed him their farms as payment for his medical services, but apparently no such thing occurred. As a matter of fact, he accepted things such as farm produce, a hog, a cow or a horse, as payment.

I learned that he not only cared for the white people of Flo, but that he would ride miles to the Negro settlements of Hopewell and Pleasant Springs to treat the black people as well. I met an eighty-nine year old black man in the Hopewell community who remembered my grandfather very well and told me that he was their family doctor.

I have been told that Doctor Taylor was prone to curse quite often. Some said he had a curse word in every sentence he uttered. One man told me that once, when he lost a patient after spending several days at his bedside, he kicked his medical bags (which were saddle bags that were carried across his horse behind his saddle) clear across the room while saying something like, "Get away from me, damn you; you couldn't save this man!"

I also heard that Dr. Powell (who practiced medicine in Centerville for over forty years) once told one of his own family members that Doctor Taylor was not a "real licensed doctor." This was resented by some members of my father's family. They felt much better years later when my sister discovered that Doctor Powell was wrong and she could prove it. She had obtained a copy of the number of Doctor Taylor's license to practice medicine from the Texas Medical Association. Only one copy of the license was ever issued.

Another questionable thing I heard about Doctor Taylor was from a member of his own family. Doctor Taylor had neighbors named Jeff and Emma Page, who lived about a mile away. Emma had an old sow that ran out on the open range and would come by Doctor Taylor's place every day or two looking for something to eat. Doctor Taylor, who considered the sow a nuisance, had my father kill the sow one day. Then they butchered her and hung her in his smoke house. Several days later Emma came riding up to Doctor Taylor's place looking for her sow. When she asked him if he had seen her, he lied, replying, "No, Miss Emma, I haven't seen your sow for a couple of weeks now." She saw smoke rising from the smoke house, but failed to ask what kind of meat Doctor Taylor was smoking at the time.

Some people said that Doctor Taylor was mean to his children. His six daughters would be playing in a group around their mother when one of them would see him coming and cry out, "Here comes Pa." The girls then scattered like quail. When he came into the house, not one of his girls was in the room he occupied.

When my father was eighteen years old he married my mother and they lived for a while with Doctor Taylor. Doctor Taylor was an early riser and one morning he approached my parent's bed and demanded that my father get out of bed and get to work. My father refused and he wouldn't let my mother get out of bed either. A few minutes later Doctor Taylor stood on their bed and proceeded to kick his son. My parents moved out of the doctor's house that day.

Doctor Taylor was pretty strict with his sons, Lee and O K (my father). He liked to be the "man in charge," and was quite willing to exploit his sons. One time he had my father raise a crop on one of his places. My father's share was to be one-third, Doctor Taylor's daughters' share was to be one-third and Doctor Taylor was to get one-third. This was sharecropping at its worst. When my father took a bale of cotton to the cotton gin in Oakwood in the fall, Doctor Taylor called the gin and asked them to withhold payment for the cotton until he arrived in Oakwood to collect the money.

They refused his request and paid my father for the bale of cotton, infuriating the doctor.

Dr. Taylor died of natural causes in 1925 and was buried in the Taylor family cemetery in Flo. I was two years old at the time and do not remember him.

All that remains of Doctor Taylor's possessions are the several farms he owned, which are now owned or have been sold by his descendants, and his personal belongings. His belongings that remain include his saddle bags (now fallen apart), an ironstone vessel in which he mixed medicines, two medical containers that have bottles and vials with medicine still in them (one labeled "cannibus"), bottles from his saddle bags, a few medical instruments, his eyeglasses and a Celluloid collar that he wore.

After Doctor Taylor's first wife died in 1899, he married my grandmother within four months. He was forty-six years old at the time and she was twenty-four. He had four children by his first wife and eight by his second wife. His descendants are scattered all over Texas now, but I know very few of them, and the ones I know are in their eighties.

15

BEATING THE SNAKE

My grandmother, Aunt Matt (Pate) Raines, was a jolly soul all her life. She was a midwife who must have delivered a hundred babies around Flo and loved to help poor families in need. She also loved kids and had eleven of her own from two different husbands.

Aunt Matt (we called her Granny Matt) was a Christian and went to church at every opportunity. She was always inviting the local preachers to her home for Sunday dinner and to spend the night if they weren't asked by others in the community.

One of the church activities she enjoyed immensely, as did most of the other older women of the community, was going to the annual revival meetings, sometimes held in the church and sometimes outside the church under a brush arbor. A brush arbor is a scaffolding that is erected with brush placed to keep the hot sun off the congregation. Aunt Matt and all her friends attended the nightly church services at the revival, sometimes for as many as seven nights in a row.

During one of the outdoor services, a snake was found near the brush arbor and was killed with a club by one of the men in the congregation. Although it didn't disrupt the services, everyone became wary and began to look around the ground quite carefully before sitting down in one of the folding chairs under the arbor.

One night, several days after the snake had been killed, Aunt Matt was sitting with her friends under the arbor listening to the preacher. She wore stockings that she "rolled", that is, she did not use garters to hold them up. Without noticing it, one of her stockings had fallen down her leg to the point that it was down around her shoe. The stocking happened to get hooked on a small black root that was on the ground under the arbor. She suddenly started screaming, kicking and shouting "Snake! Snake! Snake!" while pointing to her foot and stocking snagged on the tree root.

The area under the arbor suddenly became very busy, with people running in every direction. Even the preacher jumped onto one of the folding chairs to avoid the "deadly snake."

Aunt Bell Lathrop, another old timer in Flo, grabbed a club and began to beat the black tree root into a pulp, thinking it was a snake that had hold of Aunt Matt's foot and wouldn't let go. She nearly crippled Aunt Matt because part of the time she was hitting her foot with the club.

It took about a half hour to restore things to normal and everyone decided that the revival meeting had been a total success that night already, and wouldn't let the preacher take up his sermon where he had been interrupted.

That was the same night that Aunt Matt rode home in her wagon with all her kids and neighbor's kids sleeping all around her. She didn't realize that she had left one of her baby sons sleeping on a bench at the church house until she was home. She rode the wagon back to the church and found him sound asleep on his bench in the empty church never knowing that she had abandoned him.

Aunt Matt never again drove off and left one of her kids at church. She did, however, get home one night after a party and put her kids to bed, only to discover the next morning that some boys had switched the clothes on a couple of babies and that she had kept another family's baby overnight.

My mother, Aunt Matt's daughter, told me years later that she firmly believed her mother had deliberately hooked her stocking on the tree root under the arbor and started screaming just to liven up the church services for a change. She was known to pull such stunts from time to time.

16

BROTHER CHASE

Shortly after the turn of the century, between about 1905 and 1910, there was a circuit-riding Baptist preacher named Brother Chase who would come through the Flo area each year, preaching at the various little churches. He might spend as long as a month in Flo before moving on. Sometimes he came to Flo alone, but in other years he would bring his wife along.

Brother Chase was considered by the Flo area people to be an authority, if not indeed a genius, when it came to religion. He not only knew his Bible, but he had a set of great books on different religions of the world and was well read in religious theology. Everyone in the Flo community agreed, however, that Brother Chase didn't have a lick of common sense and that he was very eccentric when it came to everyday affairs.

When he came to the Flo area he would spend a night or two at some farmer's place, then move on for a night or two at a neighbor's house. He sometimes stayed at the homes of both my sets of grandparents.

Brother Chase had a long beard, which frightened many of the kids. He rode around the countryside selling Bibles and other religious articles. He sold the parents little religious books for their children. The children loved the books, if not Brother Chase, for they had colored pictures in them. He once told my mother, when she was five years old, that he would give her one of the little books if she would give him a kiss. Needless to say she never got her book, because she flatly refused to kiss him.

When Brother Chase arrived at someone's home, intending to spend at least one night there, he would usually say to the housewife, "Now, don't go to any special trouble for me; just cook several pies, preferably apple, some hot biscuits and fry up a chicken or two." As he was eating he could be seen slipping biscuits into his pockets for eating later on the road.

One time Brother Chase brought his wife to Flo with him and after one of the services at the Flo church he went to get his horse and ride it back to where his wife was waiting for him. Her plan was to ride behind him on his horse so she was standing on a "style block." A style block was a raised platform, either manufactured from boards or perhaps a section of a log about three feet long, that a woman stood upon before mounting a horse. The horse would be ridden or led up to the style block and the woman would merely sit down on the horse in the sidesaddle manner. Very few women actually straddled a horse in those days. After Brother Chase got on his horse he rode right past his wife standing on the style block waiting for him and disappeared up the road.

There was a great deal of brush and woods in the Flo area in those days, as there is today, and one could easily get lost on the one-lane, dirt, wagon roads. Brother Chase didn't have a prayer of understanding where he was on these roads, so he carried along strips of cloth which he would tie to the trees and brush along his route to show him how to make his return journey.

Before long the Flo boys began to play tricks on Brother Chase because of his inattention to everyday things. In addition to following him around removing his strips of cloth from the bushes and trees, they would turn his saddle around on his horse while he was preaching a sermon in the local church. It is said that he actually mounted his horse, facing the wrong direction, at least once or twice as a result of the boys' pranks.

The local, permanent preacher in Flo in those days was Brother Enoch Parrish, who must have held services there for forty years. Brother Chase stayed at his house many times when he came to Flo. It is said that Brother Parrish received Brother Chase's extensive library of religious books upon Brother Chase's death.

17

FISHING THE CUTOFF

"In the early nineteen hundreds, around 1910 I suppose, Henry Moore, Nealey Frazier, and Newt Boykin decided they would go fishing on Buffalo Creek, about five miles northeast of the Flo crossroads," said Evan Moore, the storyteller. "It was along about June in a terribly dry year. All the men had their crops "caught up" and they did not need to do any more work on them for a while and were content to let them grow and mature.

"They went to the creek in a wagon pulled by a team of mules. As they were descending the hills into Buffalo Creek bottom, they kept meeting wild-eyed, high-headed cattle coming out of the bottom up into the hills. Henry suspected that something was wrong in the bottom, but couldn't imagine what it could be.

"They headed for a place on the creek called "The Cutoff." The creek had once formed a loop about one-fourth mile across but had later cut across this loop so the old creek bed of the loop was dry and the creek water now ran through the shorter route, the cutoff.

"The fishermen came to the old loop in the creek and crossed the dry creek bed and continued on until they came to the cutoff where they set up camp.

"They set out their hooks in the creek and sat around camp waiting for the fish to bite. Sometime in the afternoon they began to see hundreds of squirrels in the area. There were squirrels in every tree and they seemed to be scurrying about frantically. One of the men had a shotgun and a pistol with him and he fired all his shotgun ammunition at the squirrels, killing a dozen or so of them. He then began to fire his pistol at them but was not very successful with it. They skinned the squirrels, cut them up and began to fry some of them for supper (they were a delicacy back in those days and are still eaten by people in Flo). They also used some of the squirrel meat to bait their hooks.

"After dark the men went to bed in the wagon, which was covered by wagon sheets made of canvas. About midnight there came a bad rain, what folks in Flo call a "gulley washer." Thunder and lightning were crashing all around them and the rain was coming down in torrents. Soon the rain changed into hail and built up to a few inches deep around the wagon. Further up the creek it hailed much harder, accumulating to a depth of more than a foot. It is said that the local people used the hail for several days for making ice cream. There was no ice or refrigeration available at Flo then.

"During the night, the creek water grew so high that it overflowed the creek banks. Of course it filled the formerly dry creek bed in the creek loop to a depth of over six feet. The fishermen were now completely surrounded by water, the cutoff on one side and the loop on all other sides. The creek continued to rise until all the area inside the loop, including where the wagon was located, was under a foot of water.

"The men were afraid the wagon, as well as the team, were about to be washed away. They bolted from the wagon and released the mules, who promptly swam the creek to get to higher ground, then went home. The fishermen then climbed trees to escape the rising water. Nealey and Newt could swim, but refused to leave Henry who couldn't swim a lick. During all this time lightning was flashing in their faces and thunder was assaulting their ears while the rain was coming down hard and fast. Henry reported later that before they all left the wagon they had filled their pockets with biscuits, left over from their supper. He later wondered what had prompted them to do this.

"An hour later daylight came upon this very wet world. The wagon was still standing where they had camped and Henry, Nealey, and Newt were still up their trees. The creek had not yet shown any signs of dropping its water level.

"At noon some of the Raley boys, who lived a short distance up the creek from the cutoff, came down to the creek to work on one of their downed fences. At about the same time one of the fishermen's wives and her daughter arrived at the creek area looking for the fishermen. Their mules had arrived home and alerted her that the men were in trouble. She told the Raley boys about the fishermen and asked them if they had seen them.

"'There's no doubt about it,' said one of the boys, not being well trained in social graces, 'they all drowned.' When the wife and daughter heard this they became hysterical and started crying and wailing. 'I've changed my mind,' said the boy, 'maybe they didn't drown.' I'm sure this last statement was of great comfort to the woman and her daughter.

"The word spread quickly and soon other men, some of them on horseback, appeared to try to help. My father, Jack Moore, who was Henry Moore's uncle, was there on his horse. The men rode up to the creek at the loop and yelled and were promptly answered by Henry, who had by now left his tree. The creek had dropped to the point there was no standing water where the wagon was located, although the cutoff and the loop creek beds were still full of deep water, running fast.

"The men on horseback helped Nealey and Newt across the creek using ropes, and finally talked Henry into venturing out into the creek water up to his waist. They then threw him a rope and further coaxed him into tying it around his chest just under his arms. They then asked him to start trying to swim the creek. He flatly refused, being deathly afraid of the water. One of the men on a horse hooked the rope around his saddle horn and gently dragged Henry into the current. He went under immediately. The horseman decided he had nothing to lose, so spurred his horse away from the creek, dragging Henry along the bottom and up the bank, covered with mud and mad as hell. When Henry stopped gasping and spitting up water, he was ready to fight then and there. They finally calmed him down, but he accused them of trying to drown him and never did forgive the man on the horse.

"Later, the men dragged the wagon across the creek and everyone went home. The incident wasn't forgotten because here I am telling you about it eighty-three years later. If you put it in print, the story may still be around a hundred years from now after you and I are gone and have been forgotten."

18

THE BLUE BABY

One day I visited Lois and Colonel Moore in Flo, to talk about the good old days. Lois gave me a few sheets of paper as I prepared to leave. Later, when I looked over the papers, I found that each of the six sheets contained a typewritten story. Lois is a literary person and has written many stories over the years, including information on two families that appears in the Leon County, Texas history book published for the Texas Sesquicentennial in 1986.

All of Lois' stories are either true, based upon her own personal experience and memory, or they are her interpretation of stories that have come to her from others, primarily her older relatives and friends.

One of the six stories that she had given me was entitled "WHEN RANDOLPH DIED." I liked the story so well that I rewrote it (with some slight embellishment), gave it a new title, and include it in this book.

"Many of the children born here in Flo before about 1920 failed to survive their first five years of life due to the primitive conditions everyone lived under in those days," said Lois. "There was a lack of sanitary facilities, proper medication, adequate food and appropriate clothing back then. Even the doctors were inadequately trained, lived miles away, and could not be contacted by telephone. When finally reached they had to ride horseback or in a buggy over miserable roads to get to the patient.

"My husband's older brother, Randolph Moore, was born in 1908. That fact alone put him in jeopardy. A couple of years later, he became critically ill with what was then called "Typhoid Pneumonia. " This was in the days before there were screens for windows and doors, running water, inside bathrooms and all the other things that now keep us healthy.

"Randolph was taken care of and treated with the standard home remedies by his parents and grandmother, but his condition worsened. Finally, the family decided to send for Dr. Taylor. He came in a buggy from his home a mile or so away and treated Randolph as best he could. It didn't seem to help and Randolph's condition worsened. Doctor Taylor visited him a few more times during the following days, but the situation was considered hopeless and Randolph went into a coma.

"After a while Randolph appeared to have died. No sign of breathing was seen, even when a mirror was held close to his face to detect his breath, the standard practice back then to verify a death.

"Brother Lige Berry, a local Baptist minister, was sent for. He arrived on horseback and had a jug of home-made blackberry wine under his arm when he walked in. He checked Randolph carefully, then asked that a tub of warm water be brought to the boy's bedside. When this was done he emptied half of the full jug of blackberry wine into the water, set the jug aside, lifted Randolph from the bed and placed him in the tub with only his head above the water. In the meantime, Randolph's parents and grandmother and perhaps others who had come to offer their condolences, were eyeing Brother Berry with great consternation, wondering what he was doing.

"Brother Berry asked for a straight-backed chair and a teaspoon. He placed the chair beside the tub, sat down in it, looked around, and said, 'Let me and the boy have peace and quiet, please, for we have Godly things to talk about.' Everyone left the semi-dark room where Brother Berry was seated and closed the door, but not all the way, for they needed to observe this man's strange behavior from time to time.

"They could hear Brother Berry mumbling and, upon looking through the crack in the door, could see that he was praying. They soon saw him pour two drops of the blackberry wine into the spoon and place it upon Randolph's apparently lifeless lips. He then poured out two or three teaspoons of the wine and drank it himself. He repeated this operation every ten minutes or so throughout the rest of the afternoon, mumbling his prayers all the while.

"After several hours a baby's cry came from the room. The door opened and Brother Berry came out, none too steadily, presumably from sitting too long in the chair, his lips blue, carrying the empty jug on one finger. Without saying a word about the power of the Lord, or what faith in Him can do, he mounted his horse and rode away.

"In the meantime the women were lifting the crying, dark-blue baby out of the tub, and were discussing various methods they intended to use to make a white baby out of this blue baby.

"Randolph survived and lived another sixty-two years, dying in 1972. It is common knowledge around Flo that he detested the taste of blackberry wine until the day he died."

19

THE CROCUSES

Evan Moore, my most valuable source of stories, took me to his ranch located at the intersection of Wheelock Creek and Buffalo Creek, five miles northeast of Flo. His ranch covers about twelve hundred acres, much of it brush and trees.

We were driving along one of the primitive roads through the woods when I saw, off to one side, what appeared to be a row or several clumps of crocuses. Crocuses don't grow wild in the woods of Leon County unless someone plants them there and then abandons them. I told Evan to stop his truck so that I could get some photographs of the plants.

"Where did these crocuses come from?" I asked Evan after taking the photographs.

"They are the last remaining evidence that a family named Crim lived here where this brush and these trees are located. There is no longer any sign of the shack they lived in, not even the fireplace. Someone must have hauled away the fireplace rocks years ago."

"When did they live here?" I asked.

"I believe it must have been around 1915, a few years before you and I were born."

"Tell me about them," I said. I was already saddened by the thought that this family lived and suffered here in this wilderness and left nothing to show that they ever existed except a patch of crocuses that they planted, some seventy-seven years ago and that faithfully bloom each spring.

"Some ten or fifteen years after the turn of the century," Evan began the story, "a man named Crim bought 135 acres of land here in the Wheelock Creek/Buffalo Creek bottom. He was a rather young man, perhaps about thirty years old. He had a wife about his own age and a daughter about ten years old. They were back-country people, no doubt uneducated, ignorant, and dirt poor.

"They built a little log shack right here where we are standing, where the crocuses still bloom every spring. They cleared two or three acres of trees and brush off the land near the cabin. You can't tell where the cleared area was now because the trees and brush have grown back in the last eighty years. They also cleared a few acres about three hundred yards from here in the creek bottom, near Buffalo Creek. This cleared area was next to a small pond which some folks call 'Green's Pond' which fills up with water every spring.

"The Crim family lived in this cabin, miles from their nearest neighbor, for two or three years. It had to have been a miserable place, especially in the winter, because they had no money to build a proper cabin. Mr. Crim would ride a wagon to Buffalo, ten miles away, once a month to get some basic ingredients for cooking, such as sugar, salt, pepper, flour, corn meal, syrup (they raised almost all of their food) and other supplies, but his wife and daughter never left the place. I can believe that theirs was an extremely Spartan existence with few comforts and little beauty to be found. I like to believe that Mrs. Crim and her daughter planted the crocuses you see here in some desperate attempt to bring some beauty and color into their miserable lives. Let's hope they loved and cared for each other which would have made their lives bearable.

"After about three years, the Crims abandoned the crude cabin and built a better place, a small square house, a couple of hundred yards back up the road we just came over. It was near where you saw the huge hickory trees in the field. They cleared the area around the house and the hickory trees out to a distance of one hundred yards or so in all directions. I now plant oats in this field.

"The house they built was rather unique in that it was built about seven feet above the ground, resting on square beams that Mr. Crim had hand hewn from logs. The house was high enough above the ground that the small amount of livestock they had, a milk cow, a horse, and a mule, and a hog or two could get under the house out of the weather. There may have been pens built under the house for holding the hogs or other livestock. No other house in Flo has ever been built like this as far as I know.

"It may have been that the house was built up in the air for another reason, other than for the benefit of the livestock. The ranchers that lived in the area began to notice that when they rode within sight of the house, while they were out looking for their livestock or perhaps just passing by, Mrs. Crim and her daughter would run for the house and close and lock the door. She would not respond to anyone who came near the house.

"Now, you're thinking that Mrs. Crim was paranoid and perhaps she was. Could it have been that Mr. Crim was the one who was paranoid about visitors and that Mrs. Crim and her daughter were merely obeying his orders? We'll never know the answer to that, now will we? Too many years have passed to find out and the answer wouldn't change anything.

"Mr. Crim was a hard worker. He spent one whole summer installing hog proof wire around his entire 135 acres of land so that it would hold his hogs and prevent them from going wild in the creek bottoms.

"A few years later, around 1920 I suppose, he was trying to clear more land near Buffalo Creek and drain Green's Pond to provide him more land to farm. I don't know whether it was in the late fall or early spring, but it was cold, rainy, and the wind had been blowing for several days. Mr. Crim couldn't afford to buy adequate clothing for such conditions and as a result he got wet and caught a cold. Several days later it turned into pneumonia.

"The family did not send for a doctor. The nearest doctor was your grandfather, Dr. Taylor, who lived ten miles away. Who knows what went through Mr. Crim's mind in rationalizing the decision not to send for Dr. Taylor? Perhaps he didn't know your grandfather would have come even if he could not have paid him for his services at the time.

"While Mr. Crim was sick in bed, a fellow named Bake Lathrop came by the Crim place on his way to Buffalo Creek to run his trap line. For some reason, perhaps because her husband was in the house, Mrs. Crim let Bake come inside. He immediately saw that Mr. Crim was deathly sick. He went back to Limmie and Sulie Lathrop's place and told them Mr. Crim was about to die. Sulie cooked a chicken, a delicacy in those days, and gave it to Bake and sent him back to the Crim's house with it. He left the food with Mrs. Crim and went on to run his trap line. When he came back several hours later, Mrs. Crim told him that her husband was doing better, but that he had the hiccups. Bake knew better so he left and told Limmie and Sulie what he had heard and seen. They went to the Crim's house, but Mr. Crim died shortly after their arrival.

"Soon after Mr. Crim's death the mortgage holder on the place foreclosed and Mrs. Crim lost everything. I believe she and her daughter moved back to Mississippi.

"There were some other Crims around Flo when you and I were kids. One of them was Albert Crim, and he was no doubt kin to the Crims that I have been telling you about. I don't know what became of him and as far as I know there are no other Crims now living in Leon County."

Evan was silent for so long that I knew the story was over. "Does that story leave a strange, haunting feeling in your gut when you tell it?" I asked him.

"Yes, it does and I suspect it does the same thing to you. I've been watching your eyes," he said, looking away through the brush. Evan knows me pretty well.

"You know, with enough effort and patience the Crim family could be traced," I said. "That ten year old girl might still be alive somewhere. She would be about eighty-seven years old now."

"It's better to let it alone," he said. "A thing like that never turns out like it should. If you found her and asked her if she remembers the crocuses that she and her mother planted here in 1915, you would probably be disappointed in her answer. It's easier to live with the empty feeling in your heart."

"Maybe you're right," I said. "We still have the crocuses to remember her by."

20

THE WATERMELON PATCH

In 1917 my grandfather, Doctor William F. Taylor, had a watermelon field (called a "patch" in Flo) a couple of hundred yards from his home on the sandflats near Midway, about five miles southwest of the Flo crossroads. The dirt wagon road between Midway and Flo ran alongside the watermelon patch.

One Sunday afternoon my father, who was seventeen years old at the time and still lived with his father, noticed that a particular wagon, pulled by a team of mules, had passed the watermelon patch twice within an hour and that the two young men occupying the wagon were ogling the watermelons as they drove past the field. He came to the conclusion that they planned to steal some of the watermelons that night. The fellows had an excuse for passing Doctor Taylor's place that night to attend the revival meeting held at the Flo crossroads.

My father got his pump shotgun and loaded it with three low-powered shells containing No. 8 shot, the kind of shells used in quail hunting. He went to the watermelon patch just before dark and hid nearby.

As darkness fell, the wagon containing the two young men came by on their way to the church services in Flo. My father saw the two inspecting the watermelons again. They did not stop but continued on to Flo. He sat at the watermelon patch and waited.

About midnight he heard the wagon coming back. By now it was a very dark night and he could not see well at all. He heard the wagon stop and knew the two young men were climbing over the fence into the watermelon patch. One of them was dressed in dark clothing and my father could not see him at all. The other had on a white shirt and it could be seen, although barely, in the darkness.

When my father saw the white shirt move downward (to pick up a watermelon) he fired at it. The watermelon was dropped and the white shirt headed at a run for the fence. When the white shirt went up on the fence he fired at it again. This knocked the man off the fence back into the watermelon patch. He went up on the fence again and was promptly shot off it for a second time. Finally, both men made it over the fence, flung themselves into the wagon, and raced away as fast as they could, flogging the mules mercilessly.

These two young men now had a problem. One of them, the one wearing the white shirt, now being stained with blood, was writhing about in the bottom of the wagon groaning and moaning, while the other fellow was driving and whipping the mules. Their problem was that the nearest doctor, Doctor Taylor, was only two hundred yards away. But the man driving the mules refused to go there for help because it was the good doctor's watermelons they had been trying to steal when they were shot. For all he knew it was the doctor who had done the shooting. The driver nearly killed the mules driving to Centerville some ten miles away to see another doctor.

The story is told that the man dressed in dark clothing that night got only three shotgun pellets in one of his hands when he ran too close to the white shirt in the watermelon patch. The white-shirted one was said to have been hit with 108 pellets, many penetrating his skin. The pellets had to be picked out by the Centerville doctor.

It was determined later that the name of the man my father had almost killed was Will Gordon, who lived a few miles back in the woods from Doctor Taylor's place. My father later married one of his relatives, Eva Gordon.

My father was always a little leery of Will Gordon after the watermelon episode, thinking perhaps that he might someday seek revenge. Fortunately, he never did.

21

THE TAYLOR GIRLS

"Way back in 1918 a couple of your aunts, Dr. Taylor's girls, were young, pretty and as you might expect, being courted by a half dozen boys in the Flo community," said Evan Moore to me. "My older brother, Alvin Moore, and his friend, Johnny Bell, who considered themselves to be the local "ladies men," liked these girls very much and were always looking for an excuse to be near them."

"One summer one of the usual revival meetings was going on at the Flo crossroads and everyone for miles around attended the services nightly, which were being held under a brush arbor outside the church. It was *the* place where young boys and girls could get together and visit each other.

"Alvin and Johnny were at the church services one night and were eyeing the Taylor girls, who were eyeing them with equal interest. After the service was over the boys asked the girls if they could accompany them back to where they lived, about four miles from Flo. The girls did not say they *couldn't*, which to these hot-blooded Flo boys meant a full fledged invitation to do so.

"The girls had come to church on horses (there were no automobiles in Flo then). Alvin had walked to church, but Johnny had ridden a little pony-sized mustang horse. The boys decided to double up on the mustang, with Alvin riding behind Johnny, and escort the girls home.

"The girls' horses were tied up closer to the church than Johnny's mustang, so they mounted their horses before Alvin and Johnny could mount theirs. With a lot of laughing and screaming at the boys, the girls left Flo at a dead run, followed by the boys on the little mustang.

"Dr. Taylor's horses were full-sized, well-fed, saddle horses and the girls just ran off and left the boys. They would get about a quarter mile ahead of the boys, then stop and wait for them to draw near before laughing and jeering at them and running away again.

"The boys followed the girls about half way home but soon tired of this humiliation and embarrassment. When the mustang ran under a low hanging tree branch, knocking Alvin's hat off his head, they gave up the chase and turned around and headed home, no doubt to the dismay of both the girls and the boys.

"Before the boys separated that night they discussed various ways of getting even with the girls. Alvin was so mad about the whole episode that he returned the next day with an axe and chopped off the tree branch that had knocked his hat off.

"The next night both the boys and the girls were at the services eyeing each other again. The girls were giggling and laughing at the boys, and may even have made some disparaging remarks about the boys fine steed and their horsemanship.

"This time the boys didn't ask the girls if they could accompany them home. After the service, the boys mounted their two horses which they had tied up even closer to the brush arbor than the girls' horses, and were ready to ride when the girls were. The girls again left Flo at a dead run. The boys rode alongside them all the way.

"What Alvin and Johnny had done was borrow two fine horses, a fast black horse that Johnny had borrowed from his father and a fast bay horse that Alvin had borrowed from his brother. Both horses were full sized, in fine condition, and loved to run.

"After the horses ran about a mile, the girls slowed them down because the horses were winded and getting tired. At this point both boys began to flog the girls' horses across the rear with their bridle reins. This put the girls' horses into a dead run again, which was not all that good for the horses or the girls either. By this time the girls were no longer giggling and jeering at the boys.

"The boys continued to beat the girls' horses until they came to within a quarter mile of Dr. Taylor's place. At this point the girls stopped their horses, who were by then wet with sweat and blowing hard, and begged the boys to leave. Both girls were crying. 'Papa will kill us when he sees these horses in the morning,' they wailed.

"The boys, having had their revenge, smug in their self esteem, and undoubtedly smiling broadly, turned their horses toward home and rode away. The girls rode on home.

"The girls didn't make it back to the revival meeting again. Doctor Taylor refused to allow them to use his horses and it was entirely too far for them to walk. The boys were there every night, watching and waiting for the girls and became very disappointed when they failed to make an appearance."

III - THE MIDDLE YEARS (1921-1940)

22

THE BILL FARRELL TRAGEDY

All my life I have been hearing bits and pieces of the story about how Bill Farrell murdered his wife in 1921 (two years before I was born) and was finally cornered and killed by about half of the male population of the Flo community.

Backwoods country people have a fascination for strange and morbid stories, and when an incident happens way out in the pine woods and brush, such as we have in Leon County, it leads to such a story which is talked about, in hushed tones at times, for at least a hundred years. The story of Bill Farrell is typical of this type of story and is still being told by the "old heads" who live in the Flo area.

I wanted to get the story, in as complete a form as possible from someone who was *there*, so to speak, when the incident occurred. I soon discovered that the proper person to talk to was Lois Moore, who lived one-half mile from Bill Farrell at the time of the tragedy. She still lives there in the house she lived in when she was a child.

"Tell me about Bill Farrell," I said to her and her husband Colonel. This didn't surprise them at all since it is perhaps Flo's most famous story, and they knew I was in Flo to collect stories about the old days.

Lois told me the story as she remembered it. Colonel helped out from time to time.

"In 1921, Bill Farrell, his wife and their two little girls lived a half mile east of here on the Flo road where the Flo Community Center is now located. My family lived here where we now live.

"Mrs. Farrell was pregnant at the time. It was so near her due date that a few days before the tragedy occurred her husband had gone and picked up the local midwife, Aunt Bell Lathrop, using his horse and buggy. Aunt Bell was a widow living nearby and she said he was very polite and considerate. It turned out to be a false alarm so he took Aunt Bell home and thanked her for coming over.

"For some time previously, the neighbors had begun to realize that Bill was having emotional and mental problems, referred to as "nerve problems" back in those days. One man, Jack Bell, suggested that they capture Bill by force and take him to a place where he could be treated. Bill's wife passed the word that she thought she could handle him and that she needed him at home to help with the two girls and the new baby when it arrived.

"The Farrells were getting their water from a neighbor's well. The neighbors were the Arthur and Allie Timmons family, who lived half way between here and where the Farrells lived.

"The Timmons family was so concerned one evening about Bill that Allie walked to our house and brought her and Arthur's children in their sleeping clothes. I remember my mother, Katy, and Allie preparing beds for all the children. Nothing happened during the night. The next morning mother tried to keep Allie and all the children from going home, but Allie said she had to go home and get the children some clothes and send the older children to school.

"When the time came for us to go to school that day, I went against my will. We took our usual shortcut across the fields toward the Flo crossroads where our school was located, one and one-half miles away. When we got even with the Farrell place, but across an open field from it, we could hear rifles and shotguns periodically firing at or near the Farrell house.

"By this time Bill had killed his wife by shooting her in the head as she sat on the side of the bed. No one knows whether she was in labor at the time. He then sprinkled lye on the front porch and told his two little girls that they should eat it, claiming that it was sugar.

"Two local men met us on the trail we were following and told us to go back home. When we arrived home my mother, who was pregnant herself, was in the front yard listening to the guns firing. My brother, Raymond, then ten years old, told us all, 'Daddy is dead. I saw him fall.' This was true to the extent that our father, Oss, did "fall" but it was because he was trying to avoid any shot that might come his way from Bill Farrell.

"Mother immediately became hysterical when she heard Raymond's words. Doctor Powell (who practiced medicine in Leon County for at least fifty years) had driven to Flo in his Model T Ford car from Centerville and had arrived at our place about this time. He had heard, correctly, that Reuben Bain, one of the sheriff's deputies, had been wounded by Bill. He had stopped at our place seeking directions to the skirmish that was going on. When he saw and heard my mother, he immediately told her to get in the house and 'shut up.' It made her so mad that she did just that.

"During this time the neighborhood men were trying to get Bill away from his house to save his family's lives, not knowing that his wife was already dead.

"While the battle was going on, a neighbor, Brother Lige Berry, slipped up to the Farrell house and somehow got the two little girls and walked with them back to his house near where we lived.

"As the men began to crowd Bill, he left his house and headed toward Flo. All the people in the six houses between the Farrell place and Flo left their homes as he approached. After he had passed the Mary Jones house, Mary returned home and placed a telephone call to Will Yarborough's home located a quarter-mile beyond Flo. Will's wife, Celia, was home. When she heard Bill was headed for Flo she got her husband's shotgun and some shells and walked to Flo to the local schoolhouse. There, she gave them to the school teacher, a man named Demp Dyce. She helped Demp get the children upstairs in the building and had them all lie down on the floor. She then told Demp to kill Bill if he got to the schoolhouse.

"By now the entire Flo community was in a turmoil and panic. The more macho men grabbed their guns and headed for the action. Other men loaded their families up in Model T's or wagons and drove away from Flo.

"Bill was, by this time, wounded in several places but he made it to the last house before Flo, Tom and Cora Boykin's house. There, he went inside, locked the door and used the telephone (or at least it was bloody after the battle was over). Between firing sessions he began tearing strips of cloth from bed sheets and binding his wounds. He continued firing while the men on the outside were trying to talk to him and firing at him at the same time.

"No one ever knew exactly who killed Bill. Perhaps he died from several wounds received over a period of time. The house was full of bullet holes, both inside and outside.

"After the shooting stopped, only two people were dead. Bill and his wife. We had no undertakers in those days, so my mother and your grandmother, Aunt Matt Raines, prepared Bill's wife for burial. I don't know who prepared Bill's body for burial.

"The following week word reached Flo that Bill's brother, Ben, was coming to kill some of the local men he thought were responsible for Bill's death. A few days later a man rode into our yard on a horse. When my mother went to the door she recognized Ben. It upset her so badly that she ran to get away. It caused her to lose her baby. It was stillborn; a pretty little black-haired girl."

Lois' story ended here and I believe it is an accurate account of the sequence of events that occurred prior to and during Bill Farrell's death.

As could be expected, however, other stories were circulated. One was that Bill was insanely jealous of his wife, and even suspected that one of his neighbors was having an affair with her. Another was that during the battle a bullet from Bill's gun "parted the hair" of his neighbor, Arthur Timmons, one of the men who was firing at him. Still another version was that the sheriff stepped into the house where Bill had holed up and shot it out with Bill.

One conclusion I have drawn from the stories I have heard about the Bill Farrell tragedy is that in 1921 the Flo community was unprepared to cope with a man with emotional and mental problems, and therefore not only failed to prevent the tragedy, but reacted totally inappropriately after Bill had killed his wife, resulting in the death of Bill and the unborn child of Oss and Katy

Hill. The Flo community cannot be condemned for this, as it merely reflects the times and could have happened in any rural community in Texas in 1921.

After leaving Lois and Colonel's place, I drove to Brushy Cemetery, a few miles away, where members of the Hill family have been buried for more than a hundred years. I searched for, and finally found, a small grave with a tombstone that was engraved as follows:

Infant Daughter of Oss and Katy Hill
November 26, 1921

23

THE MURDER OF LUKE PRICE

It took me a half-hour to drive from the Flo crossroads to the place in the woods that I was looking for. I had heard through the Flo grapevine that this particular person wanted to talk to me. Since we had never talked with each other for more than five minutes in our lives, I assumed that this person wanted to tell me a story from the old days in Flo. I was right.

"If I tell you the true story about the murder of Luke Price in Flo, back in 1923, can you protect my identity even though you may come under pressure to reveal the source of the story? " J. Doe (obviously not a real name) asked me. "I mean I don't want my name, race, color, sex, nationality, religion or anything else mentioned in the story. Although all the major characters in the story are now dead, some of them have descendants still living in Texas, some in the Flo area, and I don't want any of them causing me trouble over the story."

"A writer's sources of information, especially those who give information to TV, newspaper and magazine reporters are confidential," I said. "There have been some big lawsuits over such matters. It's similar to the confidential information between a doctor and his patient or a lawyer and his client. If I use your story, I'll not divulge your identity. Furthermore, you will have the opportunity to approve the manuscript before I offer it for publication. Is that good enough for you?"

"That's good enough," said J. Doe, who then proceeded to tell me the following story.

"In 1923 Roy Williams owned a farm he called the 'McClarty Farm' in the Wheelock Creek bottom (near Buffalo Creek) about three miles northeast of the Flo crossroads. You know the Williams family because you went to school with Roy's children, Juanita and Gilbert. Roy was a good farmer and he raised good crops. He had lived on the farm for more than five years and had gradually added to his farmland to the point that he needed help farming it. In early spring of 1923 he went searching for sharecroppers. He made an agreement with a young black married couple in their mid-twenties from the Wildcat community (a community of blacks located a few miles southeast of Flo). The couple's name was Luke and Lulu Price. Luke and Lulu moved their meager belongings into a small log house on Roy's land.

"No blacks have ever lived in the Flo community permanently (even to this day); that is, within an area of five miles from the Flo crossroads. Blacks have apparently never felt welcome or comfortable there, and for good reason as you will understand shortly.

"As spring came, the rains moderated and Luke began breaking ground and preparing for the spring planting with the use of Roy's mule teams and farm equipment. Lulu was often in the field with him, cutting bushes or clearing brush and debris. She frequently stayed behind, doing chores or cooking at their house in the morning and would take lunch and a fresh jug of drinking water down to the creek bottom for Luke in the late morning.

"Since it was several miles from Roy's farm to the Wildcat community, which was a long walk for Luke and his wife, they could not visit their friends or relatives daily, or even weekly. Luke, being a young, strong, active man began to look around the Flo area for some sort of recreation. He was apparently not always predictable, nor did he hang his head and go into an Uncle Tom (white pleasing) act when he was in the company of white men or even white women, who lived in the Flo area.

"An example of Luke's actions was the time in the middle of a hot summer day when he abandoned his work on the farm and walked cross country three miles to a store about a mile from Flo run by your grandmother, Aunt Matt Raines. He walked into the store, asked for and drank several bottles of pop, called 'soda water' back then, paid for the pop, belched loudly and said, 'If that don't kill me, next time I'll drink all I want.' He then left the store and headed back home.

"Luke had some money, either from his own working wages, from gambling, or perhaps he had borrowed it. In any event, he soon began to associate with several unsavory white men from an area a few miles across Wheelock Creek from Roy's farm. These men were known to shoot craps and either make or bootleg moonshine whiskey. Luke was a pretty good gambler and some say he won money off some, if not all, of the white men. There is no doubt at all about what kind of relationship this soon turned into under these circumstances. Luke was tolerated in Flo, even though he was a black man, only because he had some money and was a hired hand for a respected member of the Flo community.

"There are a couple of versions of what happened soon thereafter. One version is that one or more of the white men got into debt to Luke through their gambling losses, and when they wouldn't or couldn't pay him, he threatened to turn them in to the sheriff. Another unlikely story is that Luke became a little too familiar with one of the white men's wives, perhaps making some unsolicited remarks to her which were not welcome. It doesn't really matter what the facts were. You and I know that under the circumstances such stories were bound to get started around Flo to help justify what happened later.

"To make a long story shorter, one or more of the Flo white men decided to kill Luke. The story goes that several of them got together, along with shotguns, and went to Roy's farm. They sneaked along Wheelock Creek until they came to the field where Luke was plowing with a team of mules. At this point one or two of the white men couldn't stand the stress and ran away from the others. The remaining men took two shotgun shells and emptied the lead pellets out of them and replaced the pellets with wads of paper, then recrimped the shells. All the shotgun shells were then put into a pool and each man drew two shells from the pool in a blind draw. They then loaded their shotguns with the shells from the pool.

"The idea of drawing the shotgun shells from a pool was to allow each man who shot at Luke to convince himself later that he was the one who ended up with the fake shells and therefore did not help murder Luke.

"The time was now about 11:30 in the morning. Luke had been plowing a long strip of land of ten acres. The rows were about three hundred yards long and one end of the rows ended at a heavily wooded area. In the wooded area was a ravine, almost deep enough to conceal a person while standing. Luke had proceeded to the end of the rows at the edge of the woods and had turned his team to head back to the opposite end of the field. He was shot in the back from the ravine with one or more 12-gauge shotguns loaded with buckshot. He died almost instantly. The murderers slipped away through the woods without being seen.

"Gilbert, Roy's son, who was three and a half years old at the time, was climbing peacefully in a big plum tree in Roy's back yard, when the calm was suddenly broken by shrill screaming coming from the direction of the wagon road that led from the house to the creek bottom. He thought the screams came from a vicious wildcat on the rampage. The look on his mother's face told him that something was terribly wrong. Shortly, Lulu appeared coming up the hill in a wild and frantic state screaming that something terrible had happened to her man. Roy approached the house on the dead run from the direction of the barn. Roy's nearest neighbor had also heard Lulu's screams and arrived at Roy's place just in time to go with him down to the creek bottom field to check out the situation. In the meantime, Lulu was on Roy's porch being consoled by Roy's wife, screaming, 'Luke is dead! Luke is dead!' She had apparently heard the shots and saw Luke lying on the ground.

"Roy drove his Model T Ford truck down to the area where Luke was lying and loaded him into the back of it and drove to the Flo crossroads where he left him on the porch of the old Albert Lathrop store (this was not the Aunt Matt Raines store which was located about a mile away). He then drove to Buffalo where he bought a casket for Luke. He no doubt also called the Leon County sheriff while in Buffalo. Next, he drove back to Flo with the casket, loaded Luke's body on his truck and drove him to one of Luke's relative's places in the Wildcat community. It must have been quite a shock to them to have Roy simultaneously deliver not only Luke's body, but his casket as well.

"The sheriff arrived at Roy's place the following day and went through the expected routine under the circumstances. He found one empty 12-gauge shotgun shell marked '00 BUCK' and several big brogan shoe tracks in the ravine at the end of the field where Luke was murdered. He took the empty shell with him, but hinted that nothing would be done in 'this type' of case. He was right, no one was ever charged with Luke's murder. The investigation of the murder was no doubt typical of the times, made by a law officer who had never had even the most rudimentary training in criminal technology, much less training in ethnic relations. It is highly unlikely that Roy Williams was chastised for moving the body and delivering it to Luke's relatives, along with his casket, before the sheriff arrived at the scene of the crime. It was a humane act to perform under the circumstances in 1923.

"Lulu was overcome with grief for the next few days. Gilbert had grown fond of her over a period of time and was terribly worried about her. The day after Luke's death she was crying and was being consoled by Gilbert's mother on their front porch when Gilbert went to her and said, 'Don't cry, WuWu, we'll get you a new man!'

"I suppose that the Wildcat community blacks have a slightly different version of the Luke Price story that has come down to them through the years there. It might be interesting to hear it, although I have never pursued it with them," J. Doe said to me, raised eyebrows asking me the obvious question.

"I'll see what I can do," I replied. I contacted several people in the black community, but did not find anyone who could give me a different version of the murder of Luke Price.

24

AUNT MATT AND UNCLE WILEY

"Uncle Wiley Avara was a nice old gentleman," said Evan Moore, beginning another one of his stories. "He was a jolly fellow who got along well with everyone, both men and women. He liked women, of his own age, and always treated them with great respect."

"Your grandmother, Aunt Matt Raines, was about the same age as Uncle Wiley and at the time was unmarried, her second husband having passed away some time earlier. She was like Uncle Wiley in some respects, for she too had a fine personality and disposition and loved to have a good time and see others enjoy themselves.

"From time to time Uncle Wiley would visit Aunt Matt and they would talk for hours. They would also see each other at various social functions around Flo, such as at church services and sometimes at parties. They were more like friends than anything else. Uncle Wiley was definitely interested in her; however, he was perhaps too shy to make any overtures to her.

"One night Aunt Matt had a party at her house and dozens of people came, older friends as well as many young folks. Some of her older children, who were now adults, came to the party. Uncle Wiley came as well.

"Uncle Wiley and Aunt Matt were sitting side by side on the bed in the living room watching the younger folks all around them enjoying themselves. You should understand here that their sitting on the bed together was not as bad as it sounds. In those days every living room had a bed in it which served the same purpose as a present day couch. People sat on the bed during the day and slept on it at night.

"While they were sitting there, enjoying themselves, Aunt Matt suddenly turned toward Uncle Wiley and slapped him so hard across the face that he fell off the bed onto the floor.

"When he finally regained his senses, he looked at Aunt Matt, started to ask her what in the world had caused her to do such a thing, then changed his mind because a dozen or so people had seen her slap him and were watching them. He left the party, thoroughly embarrassed and humiliated and never again socialized with Aunt Matt.

"What had happened was that one of Aunt Matt's adult daughters, Jessie Bell, who didn't care for the idea of her mother marrying still another man, had coaxed Aunt Matt's youngest son, Virgil Raines, and one of her grandsons, Lee Jones, who were about eight or ten years old, to crawl under the bed Aunt Matt and Uncle Wiley were sitting on and pinch her on the legs just behind and below her knees. Back in those days the beds were high off the floor and a kid could crawl under one easily. Aunt Matt thought that Uncle Wiley had pinched her, although she hadn't seen him do it, and that's why she slapped him.

"Years later Uncle Wiley told my brother, Edell, about Aunt Matt slapping him and said, 'I don't know what in the world caused her to slap me. I hadn't done *anything* to cause it.'

"Uncle Wiley died years later without knowing why he had been slapped. Aunt Matt may have gone to her grave as well without learning that Uncle Wiley had not pinched her."

25

THE GREAT SANDFLAT CONFRONTATION

Sometime around 1925, one of the Bell brothers was driving his Model T car from Midway toward Flo, a distance of about five miles, through the sandflat country that lay between them. Along the way he met another Model T going the other direction driven by one of the Pate brothers. They came up bumper to bumper and stopped.

The reason they didn't pass each other was because a road across a sandflat is like no other road you have ever seen in your life. It does not consist of an elevated roadbed with a ditch on each side for handling the water, but is merely a flat bottomed ditch or trough pushed out through the sand by a bulldozer blade. The roadbed is flat, consists of sand, and is anywhere from one foot to about four feet deep. If you start down one of these roads and meet another vehicle you can't pass it because the road isn't wide enough. Also, you can't drive out of the roadbed because of the sand banks on each side. One of the vehicles has to back up from a few yards to a quarter of a mile to find a wide spot or turnout in the roadbed that it can get into to let the other car pass. The big question is, of course, which one of the vehicles will do the backing up?

Bell and Pate didn't care too much for each other, and neither one agreed to back up and let the other one pass. There are literally dozens of Bells and dozens of Pates that live within a five mile radius of the Flo crossroads. These families have lived in Flo for about 150 years and they are all related to each other, both within the families and between families to one degree or another (the author is related to them all--his mother was a Pate). Both families are fighters and have been at each other's throats off and on for 150 years, sometimes fighting between families and when necessary fighting within the family.

The Bell and the Pate who faced each other on the sandflat that day were what each family refers to as a "tush hog;" that is, he is not afraid of anything that walks and will fight you any time, any place. The only reason they were hesitant about confronting each other that day was that each knew there was an excellent chance that he might die right there in the sand. Dying was bad enough, but to do so without an audience who could pass the story down through future generations was simply unacceptable.

Pretty soon other old cars, Model T's and Model A's and early vintage Chevrolets, began to pull up behind the two cars already facing each other. They couldn't turn around to leave, so every car parked in the roadbed and all the drivers and passengers converged on the two cars that had stopped originally.

The noise level got higher and higher. Pretty soon everyone was arguing and threatening each other. Had all the cars on one side belonged to Bells and all the cars on the other side belonged to Pates it could have immediately gotten out of hand. However, there was a mixture of Bells and Pates on both sides, so it wasn't all that easy to decide which side one should support.

About a hundred people had gathered around the two initial warriors, about fifty on each side, and were about ready to enter into a gang fight, even though at times one might be fighting his own brother or his own father. A couple of cooler heads slipped away and went for help. One man went for the county sheriff in Centerville, and the other went for Oss Hill, who lived a couple of miles away.

Oss Hill was the most respected man in the Flo community for fifty years. Everyone went to him sooner or later for help or advice when they were in trouble (he once prevented the arrest of one of the author's aunts). He was a religious man, a patient man, and could work out solutions to problems that no one else in Flo could solve. He would help anyone, white or black, rich or poor, many times at his own expense. He was the sage of the community and when he spoke, people listened.

Back at the sandflat, things were about to get out of hand. The two original protagonists had squared off to fight, egged on by the crowd.

"My great, great grandpa fought and died in the Alamo for this Texas sand we're standing on," said one of the men, either the Bell or the Pate. "If you think for a minute that I'm going to back down from a fight with that kind of blood flowing in my veins, you're crazy as hell."

"You want to talk about guts?" the other man asked. "Let me tell you about guts. My great, great grandpa was also at the Alamo. His name was Rose. When old William B. Travis took out his sword and drew his line in the sand and asked all the men who were ready to die for Texas to step across the line, the only man there who had guts enough to refuse him was my great, great grandpa. He crawled over the walls that night, made his way through the Mexican lines and went on to fight with Sam Houston at San Jancinto. He later married, had thirteen kids and lived to be a hundred and four years old. He died from a bullet fired by a jealous husband. Now there was a man with guts and brains!"

Both men were lying through their teeth, of course, but under the circumstances neither could be blamed for trying to intimidate the other.

Just as the men were ready to start swinging at each other, Oss Hill arrived. He sized up the situation in silence and was thankful he had arrived at the melee before the sheriff did. He climbed to the top of one of the Model T's and held out his arms. Silence slowly descended over the one hundred members of the mob. Oss stood there in silence with his arms extended until the silence became absolute.

"I understand the situation that exists here and I accuse no one of being guilty of anything except the obstruction of traffic on this country road," Oss said to the Bell and the Pate that had started the whole thing. "Will you two accept my solution to the problem if I treat you exactly alike and neither of you suffer in your pride?"

The two men looked at each other, then at Oss. Neither man said a thing.

"Let's hear you both say 'yes'" said Oss. "I'll count to three. Both of you say 'yes' on the count of three so you won't feel that you caved in first. One, two, three." Both men said "yes" at the time Oss said "three."

"Now all you people who have cars lined up here in both directions go get into your cars and back up to a point where you can turn around. No one is allowed to drive forward here. After you get turned around go on to your destination by taking the ten mile alternate route by way of Corinth. You will all meet each other on this route but it will be on roads that are wide enough to allow you to pass each other safely. I will stay here for an hour to ensure that no one uses this road while you are taking the alternate route."

"Good idea," said several people as they scattered for their cars. "You've done it again, Oss."

Soon the road was completely clear. Oss stuck around the area for an hour before heading for home. He felt pretty good about the whole thing.

It was at least a month before someone had the courage to tell Oss that when the original protagonists, the Bell and the Pate, met on the alternate route near Corinth, they parked their cars beside the road and fought each other with their fists for ten minutes until they were completely exhausted. It is said that as they were fighting, each was telling the other about what a splendid old fellow his great, great grandpa was in the days of the Alamo.

26

THE SPRING FROG

I have an aunt, whose maiden name is Alpha Dale Raines, and who lives about a half mile up the hill from the Flo store. She must be more than eighty years old now, and is what the local people call a "well preserved" lady. She has taken good care of herself all her life and has not allowed the Flo community to devastate either her beauty or her sense of humor, as is so often the case in women who have survived several decades in Flo.

When Alpha Dale was a teenager she was not only the prettiest girl around the area, but she had some nice clothes which she knew how to wear to her best advantage. She liked to dress up and go places and of course that pleased all the boys in the community who were near her age.

One Sunday morning in the spring of 1925, Alpha Dale got all "spiffied up" (as they say in Leon County) to go to church at the Flo crossroads. She was accompanied by her sister (my mother) and another lady. They had to walk to the church.

Alpha Dale was dressed to the teeth in her finest dress, even wearing jewelry, hose, and high heels. She was powdered and rouged and her hair was piled high upon her head in the latest fashion.

When the ladies got within two hundred yards of the church, they had to pass a low spot in the road where water collected after each rain. As Alpha Dale was tiptoeing past the standing water, a large green and yellow frog (called a "spring" frog by the locals) leaped out of the grass alongside the road and landed on her. Alpha Dale suddenly started screaming and went into the wildest dance my mother and the other lady had ever seen in their entire lives. Alpha Dale was a blur trying to fight the frog off her with her twisting, pitching, kicking and dancing. She dislodged the frog a few times, but he was so confused in his panic to get away that he inadvertently hopped back onto her, causing Alpha Dale to continue her wild gyrations trying to escape him. In the meantime, she had staggered into the puddle of muddy water in the road and was even seriously considering stripping off some of her clothes to try to get rid of the fool thing.

Finally, to her great relief, the frog disappeared into the grass beside the road and she waded, rather warily in case he decided to return, out of the water puddle. In the meantime, my mother and the other lady were making themselves sick, all doubled up, holding their sides, and screaming with laughter. Alpha Dale was scowling.

After the laughter finally subsided, all three women spent several minutes cleaning Alpha Dale up as best they could with their handkerchiefs. She was wet from her waist down and mad as hell.

My mother told me that a certain amount of smiling and giggling went on in the church that morning, but none of it came from Alpha Dale.

27

LITERARY MAN

The year was 1932. I was only nine years old, but I remember it well. It was the year that my Uncle Leslie, the only literary man on either side of my family, undertook the task of showing my father the proper way to kill a meat hog.

It was a Saturday morning in November, and the first miserable, blue-whistling "norther" of the season had blown south across East Texas at daylight, dropping the temperature by thirty degrees, half paralyzing us with the shock. We kids had to search for shoes and socks that had lain unused since the previous February. We dressed in all the coats we could find, not just to go outside in the weather, but also to sit in our freezing kitchen to eat breakfast. The old man ate scrambled eggs and fried squirrel, while we kids sopped up cream and sugar with our hot biscuits, our usual breakfast.

"Gonna kill Ol' Grunt today," the old man muttered between bites, "weather's right." We four kids practically snapped to attention with excitement. Hog killing day was a special occasion each year that involved all sorts of rites strange to big-eyed country kids.

"Fill the wash pot with water," the old man said, looking at me, "and build a rip-roarin' fire under it to make it boil. You gals sharpen all the butcher knives for scraping off his hair," he said to my mother and older sister. "I'll get the steel barrel ready for dippin' him."

While I was drawing water out of our dug well with a rope and bucket and dumping it in the black iron wash pot in the yard, I watched my old man go to the barn a hundred yards away and roll an empty fifty-gallon steel barrel up to a point a couple of feet from the wash pot. He got a spade and dug a hole about two feet deep in the ground then put the closed end of the barrel into the hole, tipping the barrel sideways so that the open end was just above ground level.

"What you tippin' it for, Pa?" I asked as I lit the fire all the way around the wash pot.

"He weighs damn near four hunnert pounds. Even I ain't stout enough to lift him and put him in it. I hafta sort of roll him in and out of it," he said, for once explaining the process to me, a rare occurrence indeed.

"What good does puttin' him in a barrel do?" I have the temerity to ask in the face of the tyrant. For a change he didn't explode. I suspect he was a bit winded from all the shoveling he had done.

"I'll transfer the boilin' water from the pot to the barrel after we drag him here. I'll roll him into the barrel one end at a time. Then I'll pull him out and we'll all jump on him and scrape off his hair as fast as we can with the butcher knives before the hair sets," he said, an unexpected trace of patience in his voice. I wanted to ask him what he meant by the words *hair sets* but I didn't dare, having already, I suspected, caused him to reach his limit of tolerance with me.

"How do you kill him and git him here from the barn?" I managed to ask after screwing up all my courage.

"I'll shoot him between the eyes with the twenty-two rifle, stick him, then drag him here behind the pickup," he said, almost civil in tone.

110

When the water was boiling in the pot, the old man drove the pickup truck, with my brothers and me in the back, to the barn where he backed it up near the pigpen that contained Ol' Grunt. He took the rifle out of the truck and loaded it.

Just then a Model A Ford roadster pulled up to our barn and a healthy young man stepped out of it. He was about twenty years old, with brown curly hair parted in the exact center of his head, wearing brown corduroy clothes with creases actually showing in the legs of the trousers. I noticed that he even had leather elbow patches on his coat! I was terribly embarrassed when I looked around at the patched, ragged and faded overalls and hand-me-down clothes we were all wearing.

He was my Uncle Leslie, from my mother's side of the family, who was just passing by on his way home from his studies at Sam Houston State Teacher's College in Huntsville, Texas, sixty miles south of Flo. He was a college man, the very first from our community who had attended a college and the first from our family who had finished high school. In my eyes he was an absolute prince, no question about it. I was standing there, wide-eyed, worshiping him when he said rather casually, "I say, it must be hog killing day. Surely you aren't going to kill him with the rifle?" My heart leaped at his fine voice and perfect diction.

"Course I am. That's the way I always do it," my old man said, sounding coarse and ignorant, comparatively speaking.

"I shall do it for you," my uncle said with utmost confidence, "in the manner prescribed by the French, the same way our Cajun neighbors in Louisiana do it." It was the first time in my life that I had heard the word

111

Louisiana pronounced correctly.   I thought that it sounded funny.

My old man, who was six feet two inches tall and weighed about 240 pounds, looked way down at this uncle of mine, who was half his size, and didn't say a word.

"Bring me the sledgehammer," my uncle said to me as he proceeded to take off his patent leather shoes, silk socks, corduroy coat and his bow tie. I spent no more than about ten seconds coming up with the sledgehammer. We all moved to Ol' Grunt's pen.

"My, he's a large one," my uncle said in his cultured voice, "about twice as large as I anticipated." He rolled up his expensive trousers above his knees and hopped over into the mud of the pen. He went down in the mud almost to his knees. Patting Ol' Grunt on the back, he slowly straddled him just behind his shoulders. Taking the sledgehammer in both hands he moved it up and down above the hog's head to gauge the distance properly, like the executioner at a beheading. Finally, as if it were a mere formality, he said to my old man, "Get ready to bleed him."

He brought the hammer high overhead and brought it crashing down on Ol' Grunt's head. Ol' Grunt let out an ear-piercing squeal and promptly bolted right through his pen breaking all the boards that made up the side of the pen except for the top one which was broken an instant later by my uncle's face. Ol' Grunt kept going but my uncle fell flat on his back in the mud of the pen, his white shirt and trousers a total disaster.

I'll have to hand it to him. He was up in a flash chasing Ol' Grunt across the barnyard. He leap-frogged onto his back again, once more raising the hammer high, almost like a victory sign.

112

Ol' Grunt had been raised in a foot of mud and his ankles were weak. When he hit the hard ground outside the barnyard his feet couldn't support his body, especially with a young dandy on his back, so all his ankles and hocks began to buckle with every step. I've never seen a hog on ice but I'm sure that's what he looked like.

My fading hero brought the sledgehammer down again and again on Ol' Grunt's head. The skull must have been too thick and perhaps protected by too much fat for all he managed to do was put out one of Ol' Grunt's eyes and shake him up a bit.

Ol' Grunt didn't know where he was going, of course, but as luck would have it he crippled along in a wide arc, like an old man with corns on his feet, toward the pot and barrel that we had prepared for him. My uncle kept falling off and jumping back on him in his efforts to bring him down. Finally, Ol' Grunt came to a stop, his belly flat on the ground, near the wash pot. My old man calmly stepped forward and shot him graveyard dead with the rifle.

My uncle was aghast. "Why did you shoot him?" he demanded, looking up into my old man's face. "I brought him here to the pot to kill him for you!"

My old man looked down with his thundercloud face at my uncle. "You owe me a twenty-two bullet," he said in his redneck voice. "Bring it by here tomorrow on your way back to your fancy college where they teach you how to kill a meat hog--in the French manner, of course."

I give my uncle full credit. He turned without saying another word and in his bare feet and muddy clothes, his pants legs still rolled above his knees, hobbled back to his Model A Ford and drove away, shaking his head all the while.

The next day I saw him stop at our mailbox on his way back to Huntsville. I went to the box and found a single piece of fine bond paper, folded in the middle, with a .22-caliber bullet taped to it near the top. Beneath it in a beautiful flowing script was my uncle's message. It proved to me forevermore that he was a truly literary man. It read: "O thou of little faith, wherefore didst thou doubt? Matthew 14:31."

28

THE BATH

I had just finished recording a story that Evan Moore told me about roping a wild sow when his wife, Opal, told me another story. I kept the recorder going.

"When I was a kid there was a couple that lived close to us named Bud and May Smith. For some reason or another they separated for a while and Bud came to live with us. He and my father, Bake Lathrop, were raising a crop together. In addition to Bud there were three teen-age boys that also lived with us, who were relatives of our family. One of the teen-agers was Woodrow Bell, my mother's youngest brother.

"All the men and boys worked in the fields from sunup to sundown every day. The boys went swimming in Beaver Dam Creek near our house nearly every day about dark. This kept them relatively clean as a consequence. They swam in a large pool that formed after the boys dammed up the creek. However, Bud would never go to the creek with them as he was older and he apparently detested bathing. His excuse was that he couldn't swim a lick.

"One strict rule that my mother had was that everyone, both the men and women, had to bathe every Friday evening and put on clean clothes. She did the washing on Saturday morning and needed to wash the dirty clothes that had been worn all week.

"Both the men and women bathed in the creek (at different times, of course) because we had no water well near the house. As a matter of fact, water was scarce and our cooking and drinking water was hauled from the creek to the house in a barrel on a sled pulled by a mule. It was only logical that the bathing and clothes washing take place at the creek instead of at the house.

"Bud was not bathing himself, either weekly or even monthly. He would take his clean clothes with him down to the creek and while the boys were bathing he would merely take off his dirty clothes and put on his clean clothes.

"Tommie, our mother, began to smell some unpleasant odors when she was around Bud and asked Woodrow if Bud was bathing on Friday evenings. When she found out he was not bathing she, like the pioneering type woman she was, jumped Bud about it. It didn't help. He still refused to bathe.

"I'll never know whether Tommie put the boys up to it or not, but one Friday evening when Bud had removed his clothes down on the bank of the creek, he looked up and saw three naked teen-age boys making a run at him. To his horror he saw a bar of lye soap in each boy's hand. They chased him for about an hour through the trees, brush, bushes, briers, and swamps. All their bodies were covered with scratches and bruises and some were bleeding from the punishment they had taken. They were just about to catch him when he dived into the creek into the very hole of water they always bathed in, swam under water halfway across it, popped to the surface, swam on the surface the rest of the way like an Olympic swimming champion, ran up the bank on the opposite side, grabbed his clean clothes and disappeared into the brush.

"Bud left that day and never came back to live with us. He searched for and found his estranged wife, May, and coaxed her into coming back to live with him."

29

THE PSEUDO-HANDICAP

One born and raised during the 1920's and 1930's in the pine and scrub oak country around Flo could have easily convinced himself that he had little chance to become a real success in the modern world. He could have believed that his lack of a first class education, through high school, along with the poverty he and his family endured during those years, had put him to such a disadvantage that he could never recover to compete successfully.

Let us suppose that I, personally, felt this way and had come to such a conclusion. The moment that I expounded my views in writing, I would be expected to provide the reader with my rationale for such a position. My plan here is to give you some reasons that I might use in coming to such a conclusion.

If you spend your first eighteen years in an educational system like Flo offered during those years, you can never recover from it, or "catch up" no matter how much later schooling you get or how many books you read. It's like chasing your youth after you've lost it. It simply can't be found.

To enter a great university, even in 1946, such as the University of Colorado (as I did), without ever having had a single class in Physics, Chemistry, Trigonometry, Calculus, Art, Music, Shop, Latin, Social Studies and a dozen other basic subjects that are taught in decent high schools, or without ever having had access to a library, or without having been introduced to at least some of the world's great literature, is a challenge to say the least.

Even if you work hard and graduate with honors, you are still handicapped for later things that will surely come your way in life.

I'll give you an example. I have a friend, born and raised in poverty near Arp, in East Texas, who came from a place comparable to Flo, whose life paralleled mine to some extent. He ended up with a Bachelor's and a Master's Degree in languages (he speaks and writes in several languages). When he was still fairly young, he decided to try for his Ph.D. in French at the Graduate School of the University of California at Berkeley. After spending a few years studying at Berkeley (he spent eight hours or more each day for two and a half years in the stacks of the library reading everything that was available concerning languages), he was called into the office of what he calls his "old English W. C. Fields-in-a-bow tie, pseudo-sophisticated, old-moneyed pompous department head and was told that although his grades were not bad, perhaps he had set his sights a little *too* high in expecting to get his Ph.D. in French from a place like Berkeley. When he recovered enough to ask for specifics, he was told that perhaps his East Texas country-boy background and his family's lack of money had deprived him of certain training and education in his youth that were desired characteristics of almost all Berkeley Ph.D. candidates. The last words he heard were, "Of course, if you think you have a chance, then by all means have a go at it."

My friend decided that he was being told that he would never get his Ph.D. from Berkeley, so he decided to not "have a go at it."

Kids that grew up at Flo in the 1920's and 1930's were simply ignorant, due primarily to the pathetic schooling they received. Their parents, who were kids in the early nineteen hundreds, were even less educated and therefore didn't even recognize the fact that their children were being handicapped for life by their lack of schooling.

In my family, for example, we had never even heard of the word "diarrhea." We called it everything from "bowel trouble" to "back-door trots" to "the runs." I was probably eighteen years old before I heard the word spoken for the first time and wouldn't be surprised if I asked what it meant. Maybe the Berkeley professor was right. Anyone with gaps like *that* in their education would never be able to recover to the point where he should be considered for a Ph.D. from a place like Berkeley!

Some of us Flo boys from that era like to bluster a lot and try to hide our basic ignorance by using various tricks, but we all know, deep down, that we are handicapped to some extent. I believe that if you never left Flo, for an extended period of time, you are far less likely to notice your deficiencies, than the old Flo boy who deserted the place years ago.

Based upon the information presented so far in this story, one might expect that most of the Flo people from that era are poor, ignorant rednecks today. Nothing could be less truthful. Although no doubt handicapped to some extent by the conditions that existed in our youth, we have shown a resourcefulness that is almost unbelievable. Lots of "good old boys and girls" that left Flo, and many that stayed at Flo, have made lots of money over the years, own expensive homes, drive fine cars and trucks, and have all the material things that are supposed to signify success in the world. This evidence has convinced me that the basic premise that most of us were doomed to failure from our youth is patently untrue.

So, if by chance we at times fail to recognize and appreciate some of the things that distinguish the truly successful from the not so successful, our blessing is that *we don't know the difference!*

30

THE BALKING HORSE

In 1934, the great depression was upon the land and had everyone in the Flo community by the throat, so to speak. About ninety percent of the families were engaged in a hand to mouth existence. Roosevelt was beginning to do his work to help, but hadn't yet managed to help these kind of people, who were so far down on the social and economic ladder that it appeared they would be lucky to survive, much less prosper.

Almost every man in the Flo area was a farmer. Not by any means a good farmer, but at least he owned a mule and an old plow or two and went through the motions of farming. He managed to raise enough food, if nothing more, to keep him and his family from starving.

Most of the men raised corn, which they couldn't sell because everyone in the community raised his own corn. The people themselves ate the corn, in one form or another, and fed what was left over to their few head of stock.

The corn was first eaten while it was in the roasting ear stage in the summer. Later, in the fall, after the corn was "gathered" (you don't "pick" corn in Leon County) and had become completely dry, it was shelled from the cob by hand, and taken to gristmills where it was ground into cornmeal. You may have heard the expression, "Corn fed country girls." In Leon County not only were the girls corn fed, but their brothers, parents, aunts and uncles, grandparents and all their other relatives were also corn fed. Cornbread was the most common food in Flo in those days and still ranks high as a popular food.

Oss Hill and his son-in-law "Shorty" Parker put in a sawmill near their homes a couple of miles west of the Flo crossroads. There they made lumber from the pine and oak timber that grows well in Leon County. They also put in a gristmill near the sawmill in a position where it could be powered by the engine that ran the sawmill. People would bring their corn on horseback, in wagons or in their trucks on Saturday morning from miles around to be ground when the sawmill was shut down and the gristmill was operating. Most of them had no money to pay for the corn grinding so they paid Oss and Shorty with a portion of the corn they brought to the mill.

Evan Moore, a patriarch of the Flo community at the present time, was about sixteen years old in 1934. One Saturday morning he happened to ride by Oss' home and saw a strange wagon and team there. The rig belonged to Lee Boykin, who had recently moved into Flo with his wife and kids, his team and wagon, a calf and a hog. Lee had spent the night at Oss' place.

Evan, ever the stock man, even at the tender age of sixteen years, talked to Lee about his team of horses. One of the horses was fat and looked fine, but the other was thin and poor. When Evan pointed this out to Lee he immediately defended the horse and began bragging on how he could pull a load, even going so far as to say he could pull a load better than the other horse.

They then rode on to the gristmill, Evan riding in front followed by Lee with his team and wagon. The wagon had a load of corn in it that Lee had Oss grind into cornmeal for him. After the cornmeal was loaded into his wagon, Lee stood around for an hour or so

122

talking to the other Flo men, including my father, who were at the mill. Some men would come to the mill on Saturday to "visit," even though they might not have brought corn to be ground.

Finally, Lee climbed into his wagon to leave the mill. He hadn't gone over a hundred yards when he came to a rather steep hill that his team had to climb while pulling the heavy wagon. The skinny horse balked at this point, refusing to put its weight against the horse collar he wore. No matter what Lee did, including whipping the horse in the customary manner, it simply refused to cooperate. All the men at the mill now gathered around the embarrassed Lee and made suggestions for making the horse pull his share of the load. Nothing they suggested helped in the least.

Evan told me that my father stood around the wagon watching what was going on without offering any suggestions. Finally, when everything else had been tried and failed, he went to Lee and told him that he thought he knew of a way to get the horse to pull his share of the load up the hill. Lee immediately wanted to know what he had in mind.

He didn't explain it to Lee, but asked him to disconnect the horse's trace chains from the singletree that was connected to the wagon (a horse pulls a load by means of these chains which are connected to the horse's collar). He then asked for a length of baling (smooth) wire which he wrapped around the singletree, then tied the wire firmly to the long hair of the horse's tail. He then had Lee start the team and they pulled the wagon to the top of the hill without further difficulty, with the skinny horse pulling his share of the wagon load with his tail only.

Everyone, including Evan was amazed that the arrangement had worked. Later Evan, always eager to learn a little more about stock, asked my father how he knew the trick would work.

"I didn't know it would work. I could see that the shoulders of the horse were sore and when he tried to put his weight against the collar to pull the wagon it hurt him so badly that he just refused to pull. If a horse can't push against his collar there is only one other way you can hook him to a load and that is by his tail. It was the only remaining thing that could be done, so I tried it. I, too, was surprised that it worked."

As far as Evan knows, this was the first and last case that ever occurred in the Flo area whereby a horse pulled a load with his tail that he couldn't or wouldn't pull while wearing the standard horse harness designed for such purposes.

31

FLO'S FIRST SCHOOL BUS DRIVER

I had been out for a walk around the old home place, taking a picture of the countryside here and there, when I happened to walk past Colonel (that's his nickname) and Lois Moore's home. They were both born and raised in Flo and, as far as I know, have never lived anywhere else nor wanted to live anywhere else. They are both around eighty years old now. I more or less invited myself inside to talk to them, hoping they might tell me an interesting anecdote about the good old days in Flo.

Colonel is a farmer/rancher now, but he has worked at several different jobs over the years. His nickname has nothing whatsoever to do with the military. He has always been a rather short, stout fellow and he talks reluctantly and very slowly when he talks at all. I didn't really expect him to talk to me very much, but after I prompted him about his driving the Flo school bus back in 1934, he told me the following story.

"In 1934, the school (called New Hope--and that's what it needed desperately) in Flo bought its first school bus. I remember it well for I was to be the first school bus driver. I had to hitch a ride to Fairfield, about thirty miles north of Flo, to pick it up. It was a third-hand or fourth-hand bus, and it was already literally worn out. It was an old Chevrolet with worn out tires, a knocking engine, growling gears, and terribly in need of a paint job. To top it off, the brakes worked poorly in dry weather and wouldn't work at all in wet weather. As a matter of fact, its brake linings were outside, not inside the brake drums and when they got wet, after the first puddle, the brakes simply refused to work at all.

"The school bought the bus from a used car dealer in Fairfield. I got into it and rattled off the used car lot onto Highway 75 and headed toward Buffalo, on the way to Flo. I had to experiment with the gear shift lever for the first mile or so, since there was no visual indication on the lever to show you which gear was which. I remember slamming it inadvertently into reverse a few times, which resulted in horn blowing and loud cursing from some of the drivers that were trying to use the same highway. If I remember correctly, I had at least two flat tires on the way home.

"The next morning I'm up at daylight, getting her ready for my first trip around Flo to pick up the kids.

"As you know, this area is covered with brush and timber and consists of sand with the consistency of loose sugar, red clay hills which, when wet, are slicker than a fresh-caught catfish. There was not a single foot of paved road on the entire route I was expected to cover.

"Gasoline had been brought to my place in two 55-gallon oil drums, and I was expected to fill the tank on the bus using a 5-gallon can filled with gasoline from the oil drums. Think about this for a minute. The oil drums are on the ground, standing on end and weighed about five hundred pounds each. I can't put them on a stand or a scaffold in order to put the 5-gallon can under the spigot on the drum to fill the can.

What do I do? If I had been blessed with a telephone I would certainly have called the President of the School Board, Will Barnet, and asked his advice, but I was a poor farmer like everyone else in Flo and I had no telephone. Neither did Will. Nobody in Flo had a telephone in 1934 although a few had existed here

126

earlier. It didn't matter. If I had talked to Will on the telephone he would have said, 'I don't know what to do. Use your head. That's why we're paying you thirty dollars a month!' Come to think of it, my pay was supposed to be thirty-five dollars a month, but I only got thirty. I don't know who got the other five dollars each month and I wasn't about to ask because it could have cost me the job. Just don't talk to me about how poor folks always help each other. I hope whoever got my five dollars enjoyed it as much as I would have, had I received it.

"My wife, Lois, came out of the house with our kids. Needless to say all the kids were ready to get on the bus and leave, like right now! I explained the situation to Lois and told her I was stumped about how to get the gasoline out of the 55-gallon drum into the 5-gallon can (we had no hose with which we could siphon the gas). We stood there, like the devoted couple we are, and stared at the drums and the can. We may have even been holding hands trying to figure a way out of our dilemma. We have these thinking contests like this from time to time. Sometimes I win, most times she wins.

"Lois turned to me and said, 'Turn one of the drums on its side and roll it along the ground until the spigot is facing downward toward the ground.' I didn't ask questions, I just did it. By the time I got the drum in position, she arrived with a shovel, a look of triumph on her face. She handed me the shovel.

"'Dig a hole under the spigot a little larger than the 5-gallon can,' she says to me. Her idea hits me like a truck. I stop to congratulate her, but she says, 'Don't talk, dig!'

"I dug a hole under the spigot, placed the 5-gallon can in it, turned on the spigot and bingo! I've got a can of gasoline! I filled the tank on the bus and our kids and I drove away feeling real good.

"We're doing fine chugging along the country roads, picking up kids that have come crawling out of the woods and brush along the route to catch the first bus that ever took kids to Flo school. Some of the kids hadn't been to school for several years, but were suddenly interested in education, for at least a day or two, because of the free bus ride. A couple of these 'kids' were about thirty years old as I remember.

"Our next hint of trouble, after the gasoline caper, occurred when we hit the first sandflat. Well, this bus, I learned immediately, had dual wheels on the back. Dual wheels are too wide for the ruts which had been made by the single wheels on ordinary vehicles. We stalled out immediately, the bus just standing in one place and jumping up and down on the sand.

I unloaded the kids and had them all push on the back of the bus. I had the bus in lowest gear and I was out of the bus pulling on a front fender myself. We moved a bit and stalled out again. I then used my ace in the hole. I loaded all the kids back on the bus, then let most of the air out of the tires on the back of the bus. I then easily drove out of the sandflat on nearly flat tires which were now each about twelve inches wide, riding on top of the sand instead of sinking into it.

"I parked and got out and looked over the almost flat tires with consternation. I still remember making a mental note to ask Lois why she wasn't there when I needed her to help me think of some way to solve the low tire problem.

"We wobbled up to the school about 10:00 a.m., and I was filled with relief. We were greeted with great enthusiasm by all the teachers and the kids that had walked to school. Everyone eyed the almost flat tires carefully, but not one person asked a question about them. That shows the kind of quality people that are raised in Flo.

"I made arrangements with the teachers to let all the boys in the top two grades (the tenth and eleventh-- we had no twelfth grade) take turns coming out to the bus and pumping air into the bus tires. By the end of the school day we had some worn out boys, but they were all very proud of themselves for helping.

"Late in the school day it rained. This was great for the sandflat roads, but it made a mess of the three or four red clay hills I had to climb trying to deliver the kids back home. When clay gets wet it becomes extremely slick. You don't necessarily bog down in it; you are more likely to just spin your wheels on it. I got stuck on the first hill I came to, the one that runs down to the Flo store from the west. Seeing that I couldn't climb it slowly, I got a running start and passed the Flo store going about forty miles an hour, an incredible speed under the circumstances. I got three-fourths of the way up the hill, going slower and slower, until I finally stopped, still spinning my wheels. I didn't demand it, but all the kids got out and went to the back of the bus and pushed me and the bus the rest of the way to the top. When I stopped to let them get back aboard they looked like a bunch of little savages, literally covered with red mud from head to foot.

"I got home well after dark in my dilapidated bus. It too was covered with mud. Lois met me in the yard with a cup of coffee and a sweet voice. 'Drink this, dear,' she had the gall to say to me. 'Just think, you get to do it all again tomorrow!'"

Colonel hesitates; I know he has work to do. I jump to my feet and prepare to leave. "You don't have to leave," he says, "but if you do, come back and I'll tell you about the time I took this contraption of a bus, loaded with kids, to Dallas to the Texas Centennial in 1936, and about the time Henry Lathrop and I went by train all the way to Richmond, Indiana to pick up two new buses to replace the one I have been telling you about."

ELI AND OL' RED

I believe that the idea that very poor and rather uneducated people living in a rural community are generally very friendly, generous and compassionate toward each other is a myth. At least it appeared to be a myth to me in my youth. I don't base this decision on a scientific study of the matter, but base it upon what I heard and observed when I was growing up in the nineteen thirties in Flo.

There are exceptions to almost any declaration such as this that one may have the gall to express either orally or in writing. I'm not talking here about these exceptions, but am giving you my thoughts on the generalities, a perfect example of which was a farmer I knew who lived in the Flo area during my youth. I feel that he was fairly typical of the Flo area men of those years.

Eli did not rejoice when his friend and/or neighbor got a lucky break, made some money, raised a good crop, or benefited himself in any way. He was more likely to be consumed with jealousy to the point that he would not speak to the lucky person for quite some time. If the opportunity presented itself to him whereby he could do this person a disservice, he would not hesitate to do so; especially if he thought he would not be caught in the act or be accused of committing it.

Eli hated one of his neighbors, Ellen, who also happened to be his wife's sister, with a great intensity and she returned the feeling in equal measure.

She was a redheaded woman and Eli called her "Ol' Red," not only behind her back but to her face as well. She reciprocated by calling him "Ol' Bastard," also to his face as well as behind his back.

Eli would sometimes drive past Ellen's house and if he saw her on the porch or in the yard he would stick his head out of his pickup truck and very sarcastically yell, "There's Ol' Red!" Her reply was always something like, "There goes the Ol' Bastard!" and her yell was at least as loud as his.

Eli's farm was on one side of the dirt road that led to the Flo store and Ellen's house was on the other side; that is, directly across the road from Eli's farm. One year Eli was seething with rage at Ellen over something she had done or not done (he always said that he couldn't stand seeing her "putting on airs" in front of others when she was in a crowd), so he planted a field of peas directly across the road from her home instead of the corn or cotton which he usually planted there. He planted the peas for a very specific purpose.

Ellen didn't raise chickens for market, but she had some fifty to seventy-five around her place. Chickens weren't kept penned back in those days and the chickens ran around all over the place out to about two hundred yards in every direction from Ellen's house.

As soon as peas started forming on Eli's vines, the chickens began to make their appearance in Eli's field. So did Eli. He appeared about twice each day, usually early in the morning and late in the afternoon, with a 20-gauge pump shotgun loaded with high-powered shells. He would kill two or three of Ellen's chickens each day and bring them directly across the road from her house where he would throw them, one at a time, as hard and as high as he could toward her house. Some of them would fall on the road and some would fall in her yard. The "Ol' Bastard" and "Ol' Red" would be screaming at each other as loud as they could during all this time.

Ellen had a very low-key, mild-mannered husband. She demanded one day that he "do something" about Eli. He screwed up his courage (while she was present of course) and yelled to Eli, who was standing in his field across the road, "I dare you to kill another chicken!" Eli promptly killed two more as he left the field. After that he carried a few buckshot loaded shells with him when he went chicken killing just in case Ellen had talked her husband into doing something drastic.

Eli lost his pea crop to Ellen's chickens that year, but he destroyed at least half of her flock of chickens. Both of them felt rather good about the whole thing by the time winter came. They hated each other even more after that.

"Ol Red" must have been able to stand the stress better than the "Ol' Bastard." He died in the early nineteen-fifties and she's still going strong in 1993.

THE KNUCKS

I was having another in a series of fine meals at my sister's house when in walked an elderly lady named Lorene Hood. I last saw her about fifty-five years earlier. She is about ten years older than me and was showing the wear and tear that a lifetime of hard work on a Flo, Texas farm can be expected to do to anyone. Not only had she worked in the fields like a hired hand for some sixty years after her marriage, but that was the easy part. Her childhood at home was even worse.

Perhaps she just wanted to talk to someone or maybe she had heard that I was a writing hack in Flo looking for material for this book. In any event she told me this true story.

"When my brother, Wendel, was a teen-ager, he ran around a lot with a guy named Dee Potter (not his real name). These two were just emerging into manhood and were desperate to prove to themselves and to others their own age that they were real men, ready for either fighting other men or loving all the women.

"In order to be prepared for battle with other males they decided to make themselves two pairs of 'knucks,' one for each of them. A pair of knucks is like a pair of binoculars, it's a single thing, not two things. A pair of knucks is a single piece of metal about a half inch thick that has four holes in it, through which you insert all four fingers up to the last joint. The metal below the holes is formed into a solid bar that fits in the palm of the hand. When you run your fingers through the holes up to their last joint and close your fist, there is a band of metal across the outside of the fingers. The metal causes great damage to your opponent and keeps his jaw and teeth from damaging your hand when you hit him in the face. Normally a man will buy these things, not make them. They are almost always made of brass and are therefore called 'brass knucks'.

"Wendel and Dee had no money to buy their knucks, so they decided to make them. They had no brass so they substituted Babbitt. Babbitt is the poorest grade of metal ever invented and is an alloy of tin. They had Babbitt so all they needed was a mold of a pair of knucks into which they could pour the melted Babbitt after they heated it until it was in liquid form.

"Dee stole a pair of knucks from his older brother and brought it over to Wendel's place where they got started. They pressed the knucks down into wet sand to form a crude cavity shaped like the knucks. Into the cavity they poured their liquid Babbitt and waited for it to cool and solidify.

"About the time the knucks had cooled to the point that it could be removed from the mold, our father, Dean--an old war horse--came by. He did not see the knucks as the boys covered them with their hats because they knew he would raise hell with them if he learned what they were doing.

"Dean had just learned from someone that Dee had body lice, sounding terrible here but not unheard of in Flo in those days, and demanded that he leave immediately since he didn't want his ten kids to get the lice. He would be allowed to visit Wendel again after he got rid of the lice.

"Two weeks later Dee came over to Wendel's place to visit. Wendel, knowing what could happen, asked Dee if he was lice free. Dee assured him that he was.

"About that time Dean appeared. Thinking of the lice, he asked Dee in a rather loud voice, 'Did you get rid of them damned things?'

"'I shore did,' replied Dee, thinking that he was talking about the knucks. 'When I got home I gave them to my Ma, but I can get them back any time I want them.'"

34

THE TIGER

"Two of my brothers, Vernon and Curtis, were forever picking on each other and loved to play jokes on each other," said Lorene Hood to me, starting another of her stories. "When they were teen-agers they were always trying to best each other in one way or another. We called Curtis 'Slim' because he was so tall. Even at sixteen years of age he was as tall as our father, Dean, who was about six feet four inches in his stocking feet.

"Our father, Dean, was a rough, hostile, sometimes bitter man, especially to his own family. Joking around was completely foreign to his nature and of course all his family knew he was a tyrant and avoided his wrath whenever possible.

"One night after supper, after it had gotten fairly dark outside, it came time for Curtis to go outside and open the gate to let the calves out of a certain pen. The calves had been in the pen since milking time a couple of hours earlier. Opening the gate was Curtis' responsibility.

"When Vernon heard Dean tell Curtis that it was time to let the calves out of the pen, he quickly and quietly left the house through the back door and ran around the house and stationed himself behind a bush near the front door. His plan was to wait until Curtis came out the door, then attack him like a tiger might attack a goat; that is, jump him and knock him to the ground while tearing at his clothes and biting him about the face while growling horribly at the same time.

"Meanwhile, back in the house, Curtis was delayed a bit and told his daddy, 'I'll do it in a couple of minutes.' For once, and for some unknown reason, Dean didn't explode but just stared at Curtis for a moment or so, got to his feet and walked out the front door.

"Vernon, the blood thirsty tiger, saw this form emerging into the darkness from the front door and, thinking it was Curtis, attacked with all his might. He knocked Dean to the ground while growling horribly and ripping at his clothes and biting him about the face, including one ear and his nose. Dean, after recovering his senses, yelled something like, 'Git offa me you bastard!' which caused Vernon to freeze atop his daddy, his brain reeling from the horrible mistake he had made, his heart a lump of ice in his chest. After several seconds he regained control of his muscles, leaped to his feet and ran for his life through the darkness of the night, the curses of Dean raining down upon his head.

"Knowing that he could never again return home with any degree of safety and dignity, Vernon left the family nest that night and did not return, even for a visit, for several years."

35

SANTA CLAUS IN OVERALLS

Back in the nineteen thirties, almost all the inhabitants of Flo and the surrounding areas were extremely poor. Even the most prosperous families were, by today's standards, operating well below the poverty level. Most of the people in this rural area suffered at times from hunger, lack of medical attention, and inadequate shelter and clothing.

Even more poor than the average family were those families where the father and husband was an outright drunk (the term "alcoholic" had not yet been introduced into the area). These men would not necessarily stay drunk full time, but would usually start drinking on Friday evening or Saturday morning and stay drunk over the weekend. They might work hard all week, but when they got a few dollars together some of them would spend it all on booze for the weekend, leaving no money or very little money for the wife and mother to buy the most basic necessities to feed and clothe the family. There isn't much doubt about what caused some, if not most, of this drunkenness. It had to do with the great depression as well as the low education level of almost all of the adults in the area back in those days. Drinking was the means for a man, temporarily at least, to escape from the drudgery and hopelessness of the times.

There were a few families scattered about the countryside that may have been in even worse financial condition than those headed by an alcoholic father and husband. These were the families where the father had either died or abandoned his wife and children. Such a family was usually desperate for the bare necessities of life. One might think that in these cases the relatives, neighbors and acquaintances would band together and help over the years, especially while the children in the family were growing up. This no doubt happened at times, but in most cases no such help was provided. Although everyone was poor, even the poorest neighbors could have helped by providing milk, eggs, and pork to the family from time to time. The men could have helped by cutting wood for fires to cook with and to keep warm with and by breaking up the soil in a garden in the spring.

Some of the women had to break up their gardens using a grubbing hoe and sometimes had to chop cotton, pick cotton, cut cord wood, and work in other's homes washing and ironing, cleaning house, cooking, and canning vegetables that they had furnished themselves "on the halves" so that they could obtain some glass jars for their own use in canning later. The jars were, of course, considered precious objects after they had worked so hard to obtain them. If the mother of such a family could pick up a cardboard box with a few groceries in it once a month from the local relief agency located at the county seat, Centerville, she considered herself very lucky, but was likely to be frowned upon by others who envied her for the meager rations she received.

No Flo area man worth his salt, not even the drunks, would consider going "on relief" and picking up food or clothing for his family, although they may have desperately needed it. His pride wouldn't let him. He would have been called "sorry" by the other men in the community and would have considered himself worthless as well. This pride, however, didn't necessarily extend to the point where it prevented him from spending all the family income on booze every week.

One of the fatherless families lived in the Midway area, some five miles southwest of the Flo crossroads. The father had died from a heart attack in 1932 when the family lived on a farm near Huntsville, forty miles south of Leon County. After his death, his wife and two young children along with a grown daughter and her baby moved to Midway in the spring of 1933. They lived in a small shack built from rough lumber with no two by four timbers in the walls to provide for an insulation space. No paint was ever applied to the wall of the shack, either inside or outside. The roof was made of tin. There were cracks in the walls between the boards that let in the "blue whistling northers" or frigid winds that swept across the area in the winter time. A wood burning heater that stood in the middle of the shack provided heat for the shack. The heater had two cooking plates, or "stove lids," built into its top which provided a place to cook the family meals.

This family was very poor indeed. The mother was proud as a queen and somehow managed to raise two daughters, a son and a grandson in a Christian atmosphere in this shack in the woods.

A few days before Christmas in 1935 the mother and children went into the woods where the shack was located and cut a three-foot cedar bush to use as a Christmas tree. When they got home they set it up, but they had no "store bought" decorations to put on it. The mother popped a large bowl of popcorn on the heater. She and the kids ate some of it and proceeded to thread the rest of it on twine strings. They decorated the tree with the strings of popcorn and nothing else. The popcorn she used was her seed corn that she had planned to plant the following spring. She used it this day to not only to decorate the tree, but also to feed her hungry children.

I'll now let the family's youngest daughter, a Christian lady now sixty-four years old who lives in the woods a quartermile from where the old shack was located, tell the rest of this Christmas tale. This lady's maiden name was Billie Spence and she was seven years old in 1935, the year of the story.

"Christmas eve came. A cold north wind, a norther, was blowing and the shack was cold. The heater couldn't put out enough heat to keep it warm. About dark my mother made all the kids get into bed to try to keep warm.

"My bed was a cot. I slept alone on a thin mattress filled with oak leaves which we had gathered from the woods around our place. I had a single blanket for a cover that was totally inadequate for keeping me warm, so I lay there and shivered. I hoped the night would pass quickly so that Santa Claus could come and I could get a present. You see, I still believed in Santa Claus.

"My mother saw me shivering in the bed so she tore an old piece of cloth into strips, and while I watched she took a kitchen knife and went around the room trying to stuff the strips of cloth into the cracks in the walls which were letting in the cold wind. I distinctly remember that some of the cloth strips would fly out of the cracks back into the room after she moved on. I remember thinking that there was a tiger outside the shack that was blowing the cloth out of the cracks trying to get inside to get us.

"From time to time I would awaken during the night shivering in my bed. I would look over at the Christmas tree. Santa had not yet come. I remember that mother was up at times putting more wood in the heater.

"I must have finally slept soundly for a while for when I awoke it was daylight outside. I eased back the blanket on my bed and looked over at the Christmas tree. To my great sorrow I saw that there was not a single present, not even an apple, under it: I covered up my head with the blanket and started crying. How could Santa forget? My heart was broken. I lay there for perhaps a half hour with the blanket over my head. I could not bear to remove it because I would see the barren Christmas tree.

"Hearing a knock on the flimsy door of the shack, I looked out from under the covers and watched my mother move across the room to the door and open it.

"A man I had never seen before stood in the doorway. He was a heavy set man about twenty-five years old and not much taller than five feet. He was dressed in a cap, a plaid shirt, and denim overalls that came to a point on his chest just below his chin, and brogan shoes. In his arms he held a cardboard box.

"I remember thinking, quite clearly, that he was Santa Claus and that he had been delayed by the cold wind and that the wind had blown his red Santa Claus suit off his body. I noticed that he looked around the interior of our shack before passing the box to my mother and then quickly walking away.

"After he had left we all gathered around the box with excitement. It contained, among other food, a ham. More important to me at the time, however, were the few trinkets, candy, nuts and fruit that were also in the box.

"My mother immediately began to cut slices off the ham and fry them in a frying pan. We were undernourished and half starving at the time (although I did not know it then). I remember that we gathered around the frying pan and were sniffing the delicious aroma rising from it. I got too close and burned the end of my nose when it touched the edge of the frying pan.

"I found out later that the ham and some other things in the box had been provided by Mrs. Emma Page, who lived about two miles from us. She has always occupied a special place in my heart.

"That's the end of my true, hard to believe, 1935 Christmas story," she said with tears in her eyes.

"Where was this shack located?" I asked. I thought I knew for I very vaguely remembered the shack from my youth.

"A quarter-mile from here on the one-lane dirt road that you just came over on the way to my house," she replied. It was the shack I had remembered.

"Are you willing to identify the man that came to your door on Christmas morning all those years ago?" I asked.

"With pleasure," she replied. "It was Colonel Moore, your neighbor all those years you lived in Flo when you were a boy. Colonel belonged to a Masonic Lodge back then and still does. Don't ever make a disparaging remark within my hearing about Colonel or the Masons. He and Emma Page were God's gift to me and my family that Christmas day in 1935."

About a week later I was talking to Colonel and his wife, Lois, who still live near our old homestead. They are both about eighty years old now. I asked them if they remembered Colonel taking the box to this widow's house on Christmas day in 1935.

"Of course I remember it." replied Colonel. "It seems like it was yesterday. You don't forget a thing like that for the rest of your days. The thing I remember most vividly was that when I looked around the shack they lived in, I saw that the only thing they had to eat was lying on the table in plain view." He did not continue.

After a time I asked, "What was lying on the table?"

"A small pile of sandjack acorns and a larger pile of hickory nuts picked up from the ground from under the trees there in the woods where they lived."

36

THE FISHING SECRET

Between the years 1935 and 1940 my father, my brothers and I had this fishing thing going in Flo that completely baffled all the men and boys of the community that were interested in fishing. It concerned our ability to catch lots of large fish out of a small creek, called Buffalo Creek, that meanders through the Flo area. The community's men and boys didn't know that they were being fooled, however, for they thought we were catching the big fish out of the Trinity River, somewhere east of Oakwood, twenty miles away.

Two or three times each year, usually in the spring, we would come roaring through the Flo crossroads about noon on Saturday or Sunday at about fifty miles an hour in my father's truck, an incredible speed on the dirt roads that ran through Flo. We never exceeded this speed only because his old truck simply wouldn't go any faster. As we came down the hill into the crossroads my brothers and I would be standing in the back of the pickup truck holding up the string of fish we had caught the previous night and that morning. The old man would be blowing the truck horn continuously and would have his left arm out of the window of the truck and would be pounding his hand against the truck door as fast and loud as possible. We boys would yell our heads off as we held up the string of fish, as we flashed past the Flo store and the Flo church, which were located across the road from each other. On both days, especially on Sunday because of church services, up to forty or fifty people might be in Flo and would watch, open mouthed, as we roared past.

When I think back on this antic after all these years it is a bit embarrassing because it was redneck, ignorant, hillbilly behavior at its worst.

The problem with all the fishermen around Flo during those years was that they didn't realize that little Buffalo Creek, which sometimes stopped running in the middle of a summer in a dry year, was at certain times full of large fish. The creek contained varieties such as two or three kinds of catfish (channel cat, blue cat and yellow cat) and fresh water drum, as well as black bass (which the local people, including us, called "trout"). Most of the time, however, the little creek had no large fish in it, or very few, as I will explain later.

Everyone in Flo thought the creek had nothing but perch in it and therefore the standard fishing tackle consisted of a cane pole (or a pole cut from a long thin tree branch), a fishing line no larger than a large thread, and a small size 12 hook. The locals would fish all day with such a rig, using worms or cut bait (flesh from a rabbit or bird or perhaps a piece of pork). At the end of the day a good fisherman would possibly have two dozen perch, each smaller than his hand and weighing perhaps an ounce each. The fish would be fried very crisp and would be eaten bones and all.

Perhaps once a year one of the large fish would hit the worm or other bait on the little hook and would immediately break the fishing line or straighten out the hook. For the rest of his life the fisherman would tell the tale of the big one that got away to anyone that would listen.

My father discovered in 1935, by accident, that the creek could be full of big fish at times, and what kind of fishing tackle to use to catch them.

In the late fall of 1934 he ordered a minnow seine from Montgomery Ward. Early in the spring of 1935 we decided to go fishing on Buffalo Creek. We stopped at a slough before we got to the creek and he made my brother and me go into an ominous looking pothole of water, against our wishes I might add, to seine for minnows. The hole of water was mud colored and was like a swamp. It was full of logs and grass and bushes, which were bad enough, but it was also full of creatures such as snakes, frogs, turtles and no telling what else. I remember seeing a water snake, probably a water moccasin, slither away from us through the grass. When I pointed him out to the old man, he merely said, "He won't hurt you. He's more afraid of you than you are of him. That's why he's leaving." We dragged the seine around in the mud over logs and stumps, following his instructions, and when we finally dragged the seine from the water it contained a dozen ugly crawfish (which we called crawdads) as big as your hand, two snapping turtles each as large as a basketball, and a trash fish (a member of the sucker family) called, of all things, a "Buffalo." There were no minnows in the seine. "The turtles ate the minnows," was the explanation for the absence of minnows. The old man killed the turtles, threw the trash fish in the bushes, and placed the crawdads in a gallon bucket for later use as bait.

We then proceeded on to the creek. For some reason, the old man decided to fish with a whole crawdad instead of cutting one up to use on our tiny hooks. Since you couldn't fish with a large, whole crawdad using a thread-like line and a small hook, he rummaged around in his homemade fishing box and came up with a cord that must have had a breaking strength of at least twenty or thirty pounds. He then found a strong No. 1 hook which he attached to the end of the cord. The hook looked monstrous to me and was so large that a man's thumb could easily be placed in the bend of the hook. He threaded the hook through the tail of one of the big crawdads (after breaking off his pincers) and brought the point out where the tail joins the body. When he dropped the crawdad into one of the water holes, a large fish hit the bait before it even had a chance to settle to full depth in the water. Within ten seconds he had a six pound blue catfish flopping on the bank.

That's how it all started. With an experiment that was akin to an accident. My brother and I didn't fish that day because there were no more large hooks or cords available in the old man's fishing box. He caught four more large fish, as I remember, and we did our redneck act for the first time as we went through Flo on the way home.

The following week the old man went to town and bought about four hundred feet of twenty pound test cord (this was before the days of monofilament fishing lines) and about fifty strong No. 2 hooks. We then made up about forty fishing lines, each about eight feet long and equipped with a No. 2 hook and a piece of thin lead which was hammered flat then rolled onto the line to act as a weight (we couldn't afford to buy modern sinkers).

The following Saturday morning we were back on the creek at daybreak with our forty fishing poles (which we had cut from the timber along the creek bank) and another gallon bucket full of crawdads. We moved up the creek about a mile, putting a pole and line in every hole of water in the creek. These were "set" hooks in which the sharpened end of the pole was pressed into the mud bank of the creek, while the pole extended over the creek, which allowed the hook and crawdad to extend into the water. By the time we had set out the last pole we had already caught several large fish, some of which were drum. The drum are sometimes called "sheepshead" because of the shape of their heads. When you first pull them from the water they are silver colored, but start turning red or pink within minutes. They also make a grating or grunting sound as they lie on the ground.

We spent about an hour fishing with hand held poles upstream from the last "set" hook before starting back downstream toward the truck, removing fish and turtles from the set hooks, then rebaiting the hooks. When we arrived at the truck we had about thrity-five pounds of fish, and of course we had to impress the folks gathered at the Flo crossroads by yelling our heads off and holding up the fish as we thundered past the crowd.

The set hooks were left in the creek overnight. We went back to the creek the following morning and again "ran" the hooks going upstream. After fishing above the set hooks for a while, we took up the poles and lines as we moved back down the creek toward the truck. We would wind each line on a "line board" after removing it from the pole. It was quite a load for all of us to carry--about thirty pounds of fish, forty poles, the line board, the gallon bucket containing crawdads, and the fishing box. We did our thing again as we thundered through the Flo crossroads.

We now had the secret, but we still had a few things to learn. One thing we learned over the next couple of years was that when we had heavy rains,

Buffalo Creek would rise until it was bank full, sometimes even higher, and that was when the big fish would come out of the Trinity River and up Buffalo Creek as far as they could get before the water level dropped. When the water dropped, the fish would end up in the water "holes" in the creek. There they would become trapped until we caught them or the next heavy rain came along to release them to move up or down the creek. We discovered that the first weekend we fished after one of the heavy rains we would catch up to forty pounds of fish. The second weekend we might catch ten or twenty pounds. The third weekend we might catch only one or two fish. After that we would catch nothing at all until the creek rose again.

Another thing we learned was to dump our excess crawdads into a small water tank near our house where we could later make one sweep of the minnow seine and come up with a half gallon of beautiful, white, tender crawdads, not at all like their huge, ugly ancestors we dragged out of the snake infested swamp earlier.

We kept the fishing thing going for about six years before I left home at seventeen years of age to pursue bigger and better things. During this time, no other fishermen in Flo ever knew that the large fish we were catching were coming out of Buffalo Creek, where they might catch a dozen four-inch perch on a good day if they fished hard.

I drive past Buffalo Creek now on a paved road that runs from the Flo crossroads to Oakwood. All the timber is now gone from the creek area where I fished and hunted when I was a boy. The land there is now owned by some wealthy "foreigner" (defined as someone not born and raised in the Flo area), and shows all the modern signs of so-called land improvement, fashionable conservation, environmental consciousness, financial worthiness, and no doubt makes a great conversation piece for the owner and his friends. He wouldn't know what I was talking about if I tried to tell him of the old days and asked his permission to fish in the creek where I fished as a boy.

37

THE FOX HUNTER

My father, O K Taylor, was a fox hunter for
about thirty years. He did not hunt gray foxes for their
pelts. Instead, he hunted them just to hear a pack of
hounds in full cry chasing a fox through the brush,
thickets, woods and swamps in the middle of the night.
Their barking was music to his ears.

He rarely hunted alone. He had three or four
men in Flo that he usually hunted with. Sometimes, he
would allow me to accompany him on a hunt, along with
the sons of some of the other hunters.

Each of the adult hunters had several hounds. At
times the hunters would put as many as twenty fox
hounds in the field simultaneously. At one time, O K
owned a total of nineteen hounds, albeit some of them
were pups.

Most of the fox hounds owned by the men were
called "Walker" dogs. Most of the dogs were related to
each other and were white with splotches of black or
brown on them. A few of the dogs were a different
breed, called "Black and Tans", which describes their
colors.

The fox hunters went hunting at least once a
week during the winter, usually on a Friday or Saturday
night. Each hunter took great pride in his fox dogs and
recognized each of his dogs' bark or "voice," as well as
the voices of all the other hunter's dogs. If a dog did
something "wrong" during a hunt, either because he had
grown old or was sick or for a variety of other reasons,
the dog had to pay the consequences. If he ran down

trails or roads instead of bucking the brush through which the fox had actually run, or perhaps returned to where the men were standing around listening to the race, he likely would not live until the following morning because his owner would be so embarrassed and humiliated that he might kill him on the spot. If a dog chased an armadillo, o'possum, raccoon or rabbit when he was supposed to be chasing a fox, he was as good as dead right there.

Each dog had a reputation and all the hunters hoped that his dog would improve his reputation, or at least not downgrade it, during each hunt.

All the dogs were strong and tough. They were kept half starved so they could hunt and run better. One time O K kicked one of his hounds named "Ol' Rock" and broke his hip. As was the norm, he did not doctor the dog and intended to destroy him immediately. For some reason he delayed destroying the dog (not because of sympathy for the dog) for several days. Three nights later he went fox hunting and left Ol' Rock at home. In the middle of the race he heard Ol' Rock chasing a fox, a half mile behind the other dogs in the pack. After the fox went up a tree, the men arrived to jump him out. Ol' Rock, dragging a back leg, arrived at the tree ten minutes late. O K shot him then and there. Later, he praised the dog for his blood lines and his courage, but had killed him because he wouldn't own a dog that ran at the rear of the pack, with or without a broken hip.

O K's best fox dog for years was a flag-tailed Walker dog called "Ol' Lightnin'." No other dog in the county, perhaps even in the State of Texas, could match him when it came to cold trailing a fox, or chasing it once it had been jumped. This dog could cold trail a fox that had passed hours before. He would bark only every minute or so while he was slowly following the trail, and his bark was a long, wailing, mournful cry that was completely unique and entirely different from his bark while he was in hot pursuit of a fox or while he was barking at a fox that had gone up a tree. Once the fox was jumped; that is, Ol' Lightnin' got close enough to it to make it run, the entire pack of dogs could smell the fox and all would join in, barking constantly. Ol' Lightnin' always led the pack until the fox was either caught and killed on the ground by the dogs or climbed a tree.

A gray fox cannot climb just any tree, but he will know of a tree or two that he *can* climb. The tree is always a "stooping" tree that does not grow straight up but grows at an angle with respect to the ground. When the dogs really press him he will head for his stooping tree and climb it using the rough bark and large and small limbs growing out of the tree trunk for foot holds. Sometimes a fox dog will try to climb the tree after the fox, but usually falls out of the tree, sometimes injuring himself.

Once the fox goes up the tree the dogs surround the tree and bark at the fox, which means they have "treed" the fox. Their barking is entirely different from that of the trailing bark or the running bark and even a novice hunter can easily tell the difference.

All the men (and quite often boys) arrive at the tree area and each hunter carefully notes which tree each dog is barking up. By this time the fox's smell is everywhere and some of the dogs will get confused and bark up the wrong tree. It's a sad day in the hunter's life when he discovers that his best hound is barking up the wrong tree for his dog will forevermore be referred to as a "lying fox dog," much to the secret delight of the other hunters.

The hunters then catch all the fox dogs and if there are any boys along they make each boy hold two dogs in each hand, using the dogs' collars. At this point, a "chunk" of wood is thrown up into the tree and the fox jumps out of the tree onto the ground and takes off running.

Now comes the real problem for the boys. The boy may weigh a hundred pounds and he is trying to hold two sixty to eighty pounds of excited, thrashing, fighting dogs in each hand while being dragged around over bushes and brush higher than his head and being slammed into trees by the four dogs he is hanging onto. He doesn't dare let go because his father might consider him a wimp and not worthy of ever being taken on a fox hunt again. After what seems like forever, but is only perhaps ten seconds, one of the adults will yell, "Let 'em go!" and all the dogs are released simultaneously.

The dogs continue to chase the fox and either catch him on the ground or put him up another tree, if he has one handy. If the fox is killed on the ground, the dogs are called in using the hunter's hunting horns, and everyone goes looking for another fox. If the fox goes up another tree, he is usually left in the second tree and the hunters get their dogs and go looking for a fresh fox. A fox seldom survives the hounds if he is jumped out of a tree for the second time in one night because he is too tired to outrun the dogs.

I vividly remember two things about the fox hunts. One is the way the grown men would scream at the dogs when the race was under way, encouraging them to chase with all their enthusiasm. Their yells would be something like "Yeeee Hoooo", each syllable held for perhaps three seconds and rendered in such a loud voice that acorns would literally drop off the trees in the immediate area. The second thing I remember is that it was on the hunts that the fathers in the group would first sanction their sons having a drink of straight whiskey, usually out of a fruit jar, to initiate them into the world of the fox hunter.

I must have been in fifty or more fox hunts in my youth and I have scars to prove it. Most of the hunts were very exciting, but sooner or later in the night things would quiet down, the dogs would have all disappeared, usually while chasing a fox, and I would become very sleepy. Along about three o'clock in the morning one of the men would build a fire and we would all gather around it for half an hour or so, hoping the dogs would chase the fox back within our hearing.

About four o'clock everyone would lay down on the cold, rocky ground and drop off to sleep. The fire would go out and it would get miserably cold toward daylight. No food or drink (except the whiskey) was taken along on the hunt by anyone. Many a night I have sat, cold and miserable, waiting for daylight to come and wishing that it would hurry.

At sunup everyone would get up off the ground where he had been trying to sleep, stretch, talk about the hunt, and start walking toward home or to where we had left the truck. The dogs would never return to the campfire, but instead would come straggling home about mid-morning.

I have no sons, but I do have a grandson, now nineteen years old. I sometimes think that it would have been a pleasure to have taken him on one of those old fashioned fox hunts to let him experience some of the things his grandfather experienced when he was a boy.

Those days are gone forever, of course, and perhaps it's just as well. The world offers more important things for youngsters to do these days than chase the gray fox with a pack of hounds in a place like Leon County, Texas.

38

THE BEE TREE HUNTING CONTEST

This tale begins around the year 1936 and spans about three years. It involves an unofficial, informal contest between several men and a boy that lived in Flo to determine who was the best at locating a certain bee tree in the Buffalo Creek bottom.

Several men from Flo regularly fished in Buffalo Creek including my father, O K Taylor, a man named Bake Lathrop, another man named Henry Morgan (who lived on the banks of Buffalo Creek), and a teenage boy named Reuben Barnett who also lived near the creek.

Over a period of about a year, each of these men and the boy discovered that at one point on the creek there was always an abundance of honey bees working the flowers along the creek banks. They all sooner or later tried to locate the bee tree that the bees were using, knowing it had to be a good one with lots of honey in it. They were all unsuccessful in their efforts to locate the tree.

After a while, the men and the boy began to talk to each other when they met along the creek about their individual efforts to locate the bee tree. It soon became a full-fledged contest to determine who would be the first to locate the tree. No prize money was mentioned because this was during the dark days of the depression and no money was available for such sporting events.

Normally a bee tree is not all that hard to find. An experienced honey hunter learns to watch individual bees and follow them toward their tree when they have gathered enough nectar from the flowers or water from their watering places. It may take a day or so to find the tree, however, and one must be extremely patient in his search for the tree.

So, what was the problem here? The problem was that a huge thicket, heavily interlaced with briers and thorns of many kinds, covered about three acres of the creek bank and the thicket sometimes had as much as a foot of standing water in it. To enter the thicket was a task that no one wanted to do because his clothes would be torn badly and his hands and face scratched up from the briers and thorns. Not only that, he would be almost blind in the thicket because of the thick vegetation growing all around him. He would also be standing in mud and water among snakes and turtles if he ventured into the thicket. Finally, the thicket consisted of a low, dense growth of brush, grass and vines. No decent sized tree grew in this marsh and all the bee tree hunters knew that bees love to use a tall easily accessible tree in which to store their honey. Many times their entry into the tree would be thirty or so feet in the air. Although each hunter learned that the bees headed out over this thicket from the creek, he could not locate the bee tree beyond the thicket.

The contest went on for at least three years. The men and the boy would compare notes about twice a year to see if any progress had been made in locating the bee tree. No progress was made by any of the contestants.

During the winter none of the contestants fished the creek, but occasionally each of them would go to the creek to hunt ducks, squirrels, deer or perhaps run a trap line.

One day, in the dead of winter, Henry Morgan, a true woodsman, left his bachelor's shack on the creek bank and was walking through the creek bottom on his way to cut some wood to sell. All he had with him was the clothes he wore and a double-bit axe. It was a bitter cold day. About a mile or so from his shack he came upon the spot along the creek where the bees always worked and the impenetrable thicket was located. Since it was winter, the vegetation of the thicket had died back somewhat and he could see over the thicket pretty well. He noticed some activity just above one point near the center of the thicket and upon looking closely could see that bees were working that area. He realized immediately that he was looking at the area the bees had used for years to store their honey. Being a gutsy type, to say the least, he paid very little attention to his comfort and plunged off into the thicket and forced his way through it to where he had seen the bees. He ignored the briers and thorns and the freezing water he was standing in. When he arrived at the area where he had seen the bees, he discovered that they stored their honey in a dead snag of a stump about eight feet tall. The snag had almost rotted away and was ready to fall over if a stiff breeze came along. The bees were aroused because the snag was threatening to fall into the water at any moment.

Henry had a decision to make. Should he head for home to get a bucket of some sort to put the honey in when he chopped into the tree? He decided against this because it would take a couple of hours to get there and back and it would be dark by the time he returned. He could not wait until the following day because the snag might fall during the night. He made his decision to rob the honey then and there, but what would he use to put the honey in to carry it back to his shack?

Henry waded out of the thicket and removed his outer clothes. He then removed his long-handled drawers, with the trap door in the back, and tied a knot at the end of each leg and each arm. He left the trap door open as an entry port for putting the honey into the legs and arms of the drawers.

This may sound pretty unsanitary, but it was even worse than you think. Henry, who not only didn't take regular baths, also wore his long-handled drawers both winter and summer and once he put them on he never removed them until they had literally rotted off his body. These particular drawers were filthy, since he had been wearing them for almost a year. Their only redeeming feature, as far as he was concerned, was that they didn't yet have holes worn in the arms and legs, which would have let some of the honey run out.

Henry put his outer clothes back on and waded back into the thicket with his drawers in one hand and his axe in the other. He proceeded to rob the bee tree of its honey while ignoring the bee stings he was receiving. The snag contained enough honey to fill both the arms and legs of the drawers to overflowing. He then waded out of the thicket, stuck his head through the trap door of the drawers and out the front and headed home with the honey filled arms hanging down across his chest and the honey filled legs hanging down his back.

This story might never have been told, but my father had been duck hunting on Buffalo Creek that day and ran across Henry on his way home with his load of honey.

Later Henry sold this honey to several different families around Flo who never knew that he had

162

collected it in his filthy drawers. Needless to say, he never sold any of this honey to my family.

39

THE RED WAGON

We were sitting at Claude and Norma Jean Moore's table having dinner one evening. Evan and Opal Moore, friends from my starvation days as a youth, were also at the table. Knowing how Norma Jean cooks, I had refrained from eating for the entire day so that I could take full advantage of her great cooking skills. I was about to rupture myself with food when Opal told the following true story, no doubt for my benefit, knowing that I was collecting stories from the Flo area.

"My brother, Junior, and I were born eighteen months apart. Fourteen years later, along comes our little brother, Don. Don, being the baby in the family, received great care from our parents, as well as from Junior and me.

"When Don was about three years old he had a big red wagon which he rode in while Junior and I pulled him around. One day Junior was riding our old plow horse and rode up to where I was pulling the wagon with Don in it. We decided to tie the handle of the wagon to the horse's tail and let the horse pull the wagon with Don in it. Junior trotted along the road holding the bridle and got the horse going pretty fast, so fast that the red wagon was on the ground only about half the time. When he stopped I told Junior about how Don was "flying" in the wagon as the horse was trotting along. Junior wanted to watch Don "fly" so he asked me to run along at the horse's head and he would follow and watch the flying operation. I began running as fast as I could--we were heading in the direction of home--

when I stumbled and the horse got away and ran toward home pulling the wagon and Don. Pretty soon the horse was running very fast and Don was truly flying, being up in the air most of the time and hanging on to the wagon for dear life.

"The horse began to pitch and kick trying to get away from the wagon. I saw the wagon do about three revolutions in the air with Don still in it before it crashed to the ground breaking into pieces. Don did about ten somersaults across the ground (fortunately this was sandflat country and the sand was soft) before coming to rest like a crumpled rag doll in the sand. In the meantime, the horse was running for home with the handle of the wagon still tied to its tail.

"While Junior and I were consoling Don and worrying about our fate, the horse arrived home completely winded, dragging the wagon handle.

"Junior and I headed for home, taking turns carrying Don who was screaming his head off all the way. Halfway there we see an apparition with a terrible frown on its face coming through the scrub oak and myrtle bushes that grew on the sandflat. It took us a while to recognize what it was, but finally realized that it was our dear mother, Tommie. She had seen the horse with the handle of the wagon tied to its tail and was out looking for us. She had a three-foot long willow switch in her hand. I'll leave it to you to figure out what she did with the willow switch."

40

THE SPIKE BUCK

My father was a hunter all his life and hunted all the local wild animals in the Flo area. In the years between 1910 and about 1937 there were no deer--none--in the Flo community and surrounding areas. In 1937, a single small deer, in the middle of the night, came out of Evan Moore's pasture, which is located adjacent to our farm, and meandered his way across our crop land, crossed the road that runs past our place, and headed in the direction of Wheelock Creek, perhaps a mile away. I found the deer's tracks and showed them to my father and brothers. We were so fascinated by the tracks that we spent a half day following them for at least a half mile. I found out later that this deer, or his ancestors, had been released not long before by the State of Texas miles south of the Flo area.

Within about a year after we first saw these tracks there were perhaps two dozen deer in the Flo area, which means there must have been an average of one deer for every three square miles of land. Since deer don't distribute themselves "on the average," it meant that there were no deer at all on most of the land.

Having some deer around was the opportunity of a lifetime for the hunters, including my father and brothers and I. We usually hunted them once or twice a week. We would have one hunter, accompanied by a couple of hounds, make the "drive" through the woods making all kinds of noise to jump the deer. Other hunters would station themselves along a road, trail, creek, or ridge, on what we called "stands" (each with its own peculiar name). No structures were built at the stands, but the hunters would stand or sit there, with a shotgun loaded with buckshot, hoping the dogs would run a deer past them. The location of each stand was usually determined by where deer had crossed the road, or trail on earlier hunts.

Early one morning in 1938, when I was fifteen years old and weighed about one hundred pounds soaking wet, I went on a deer hunt with my father, Travis Boykin, and Chester Albright. I don't know what Travis did to earn a living, but I believe he lived in Buffalo about ten miles from Flo. Chester had a shoe repair place in "old" Buffalo on Highway 79. The newer part of Buffalo at that time was called the "Y" because Highway 75 and Highway 79 formed a Y where they crossed each other about a half mile west of "old" Buffalo.

At about sunup my father took us in his truck, along with his two hounds, to the Flo crossroads where we turned and headed south toward three villages called Russel, Ninevah, and Malvern, located several miles apart along the dirt road. A few miles out of Flo, after we passed Bill Lee's place, my father let Chester out of the truck and showed him where to stand. He drove another quarter mile and did the same thing with Travis. He then drove another quarter mile and let me out of the truck on a sandflat and showed me where I should stand or sit while waiting for a deer to show. He then turned his truck around and drove back past Chester. He parked, let his dogs out of the truck, and started his drive. The drive consisted of his walking in a semi-circle around us three hunters on the stands, at a distance of from one-half to one mile from us.

I walked across the sandflat for about fifty yards to get out of sight of the road. I leaned against a tree and prepared to wait about three hours for my father to come to the road we were on when the hunt was over.

The first thing I heard as I stood there was several ranchers in the woods on horseback. They seemed to be about a half mile straight in front of me, rounding up their hogs. This was open range country where everyone's cattle and hogs could run together on the same ground. It was a crisp, clear morning and sounds carried very well. I could hear hogs squealing, dogs baying the hogs, ranchers screaming at their dogs, and the hunter's horns blowing, all at the same time. It all sounded very chaotic to me.

All of a sudden I heard some "flopping" sounds. That's the only way to describe the sounds I heard, like someone hitting the ground with a heavy club, or perhaps rapidly bouncing a basketball on the ground. I was not the least bit excited, for I thought it was one of the rancher's horses and I expected him to ride out past me at any moment. I remember that I expected it to be one of the Lees or the Bells, who had hogs in these particular woods.

Suddenly, two small deer appeared from out of the brush about thirty yards from me. It was the first deer I had ever seen in my life. Being trained pretty well, I raised the 12-gauge, double-barreled shotgun to my shoulder, pushed off the safety, aimed it somewhere around the two deer and pulled the front trigger. The explosion deafened me for a moment and the kick from the gun staggered me.

One little deer turned away from me and disappeared into the brush. The other stopped, standing all "spraddle-legged" as we say in Leon County, and looked at me. I was cool under fire, so I lined up on him again and tried to pull the back trigger. It was solid as a rock and would not move, the gun refusing to fire. I tried twice more, but nothing happened. What to do? That was obvious. I lowered the gun and looked it over. To my surprise I saw that the safety had been moved from the "Off" position to a point halfway between the "Off" and "On" positions. I moved the safety to the "Off" position and looked up expecting to see that the deer had disappeared. He was still standing there staring at me. I believe it was a case of two inexperienced juveniles trying to out-innocent each other.

I pointed the gun in his general direction and pulled the rear trigger and the gun fired. I saw bark jump off a ten-inch postoak tree about six feet left of the deer. I later found that I had put the whole load into the tree. The deer turned and wobbled off through the brush, out of my sight.

Let me tell you what caused my trouble with the gun. My father was born to tinker with guns. He never owned one in his life that he didn't take apart and "work on." He did more gun butchering than he did gunsmithing. On this particular shotgun he went inside it and *reversed* the "On" and "Off" safety positions. All double barrel shotguns are designed so that you push the switch on top of the stock *forward* to put the safety in the "Off" (ready to fire) position and *backward* to put the safety in the "On" (gun won't fire) position. The safety is designed that way so that when the first barrel is fired and the gun kicks backward your thumb won't push the safety to the "On" position, preventing you from firing the second barrel. My father didn't know this, of course, and his redesign caused my thumb to move the safety forward toward the "On" position, just far enough to keep me from firing the second barrel.

Within two minutes Travis came walking up to me. "What did you shoot at?" he asked.

"Two deer. I think I hit one of them. He acted funny."

"Which way did he go?" he asked. I pointed through the brush. "Let's separate about twenty steps and follow him."

We hadn't gone over thirty or forty steps through the brush when I saw the deer dead on the ground and pointed him out to Travis. We quickly went to the deer, a little spike buck, and Travis squatted next to the deer across from me. He suddenly stuck out his hand, shook mine, and said, "Put her there, Pardner."

In all my life I have never heard words that thrilled me like those words did that day. To have a full grown man say that to me, a fifteen year old kid so shy that I could hardly talk, even to him, is one of the highlights of my entire life.

Fifteen minutes later my father came walking up. He had, of course, heard the shots. "Who shot him?" he asked.

"I did," I said, proud as could be. He didn't say a word or even look at me, or call me "Pardner." Perhaps he was jealous that I had killed a deer before he had. He merely reached down and grabbed the little spike buck by the back legs, threw him over his shoulder as if he weighed ten pounds instead of about a hundred, and headed at a fast walk through the woods to the truck.

Chester met us at the truck. My father threw the little buck in the truck, threw some feed sacks over him, and we headed through Flo toward our home a mile west of Flo. When we got there I expected that we would take the deer up into the woods which came down to the back of our house, skin him, cut him up, divide the meat and then everyone would go home after a successful hunt. Not so. He somehow conned Chester and Travis into taking the deer, in the trunk of their car, to Buffalo, where they lived. This was the first inkling that I ever had that my father was afraid of the law, even afraid of a game warden.

Chester and Travis drove into one of their garages, hung, skinned, and cut up the deer, divided it and placed it in their refrigerators. They discovered that the deer had been hit by one pellet from the shotgun and the pellet had gone through the deer's heart. Obviously I had entirely missed the deer with both shots, but for a single pellet which had separated from the main load and was whizzing off to the side somewhere. After dark Chester and Travis took the deer skin, with the deer's head still attached, to some back alley in Buffalo and buried it.

The next day was Saturday and about noon Buffalo was full of people. All the farmers, with their wives and kids, came to town on Saturday. My family was also there. Travis, Chester and I were visiting each other on the sidewalk in front of Chester's store, feeling smug in our little secret, when we saw and heard a commotion in the single street (actually Highway 79) that ran in front of all the stores. Then we saw a dog dragging a deer skin, with a spike buck's head still attached, down the street toward us. A crowd of people was going along with the dog talking excitedly about what he was dragging. Travis, Chester and I didn't say a word to each other or to anyone else. We did, as I remember, raise our eyebrows at each other while trying our very best to maintain our poker faces.

There was some talk about calling Leon County's game warden because the deer had been killed out of season, but it apparently never happened. No one ever knew that not a single one of the hunters that were involved had ever bought a hunting or fishing license of any kind in his entire life and paid no attention whatsoever to hunting seasons.

Thirty-five years later, in 1973, I hit the ripe old age of fifty years and thought my life was over, or at least was on a downhill slide. I drove, alone, all the way to Leon County from Colorado, feeling sorry for myself and wanting to say goodby, more or less, to old friends before I was called to my reward. I saw this lean old man sitting on the sidewalk in "old" Buffalo in front of the store that had once been used by Chester. He and I recognized each other at the same instant. It was Travis Boykin. He looked pretty good and was dressed in immaculate clothes, clean as a pin. The women in his family obviously took good care of him in his old age. We spoke, shook hands, and he immediately said to me, "You remember that little spike buck you shot in 1938?"

I never saw Travis again. He died after I returned to Colorado. By the world's standards of today, he probably never did a single thing in his entire life that would be considered "significant," except in the eyes and heart of a fifteen year old boy with whom he shook hands and called "Pardner" way back in the old days in Flo.

41

THE COLORADO CCC CAMP

"Back about 1938, when we were all about to starve to death, several boys from the Flo area decided to join the Civilian Conservation Corps (CCC)," said Evan Moore, one of my favorite story tellers. "Two of the Pate boys, a Moore boy, a Smith boy and perhaps a couple of others all joined.

"They, along with a dozen or so other boys from Leon County, were sent to a CCC camp located in Colorado. When they arrived there for their six month hitch in the CCC, they discovered that the weather was absolutely brutal. It was winter and their camp was located in the mountains. They were stationed in the mountains above Denver which is one mile above sea level. Snow was at times a foot deep in their camp and ice was everywhere. To make matters worse they were forced to work every day outside in the weather. Their work involved building structures, trails, and such things as parks in the mountains. Their tools were axes, shovels, saws, wedges, sledges, mauls, bulldozers, drag lines, dump trucks and other things used to work in the forests.

"The Leon County boys were southern boys and the weather demoralized them. One of the boys in the camp, named George, who was not a Flo boy, was so depressed that he went around for weeks asking all the other boys in the camp if they would be willing just to cut his head off for him, or push him off one of the cliffs in the area. This would put him out of his misery. It was funny for a while, and everyone laughed at him and teased him about it. Eventually, however, it got pretty boring and some of the boys began to dislike him for it.

"One day they were all out in the woods working in the cold when a break was called. George lay down with his head on a rock and was asking some of the Flo boys to just go ahead and cut his head off with an axe. One of the aggressive Pate boys had enough of this and so he took his axe, which he kept razor sharp, and squatted down by George and asked him, 'Are you really serious about someone cutting your head off? If you are I'll do it for you here and now. I'm sick and tired of listening to your griping.'

"'Go ahead and do it,' said George.

"The Pate boy stood up, although he was somewhat bent over above George, and took a practice swing at his neck with the axe, just getting the distance right, you understand. Whether or not he did it deliberately, the razor sharp axe nicked George's neck and blood started squirting all over. He tried to jump up, but the Pate boy held him down with a knee on his chest.

"'You're going to have to lay here and hold still if you expect me to finish cutting your head off,' said the Pate boy.

"George finally fought himself free of the Pate boy and ran around holding his bloody neck screaming for the leaders of the work crew to take him to the doctor. He spent a week in the infirmary while his wound was healing.

"When he finally came back to work on the crew, he never again invited any of the other boys, especially the Flo boys, to take him out of his misery by killing him."

174

42

THE WOODSMAN

There was a fellow that lived in Flo for many years that no one ever quite understood. His name was Henry Morgan (not his real name) and it was said and believed that he jumped off a pirate ship in Galveston Bay before the turn of the century and had somehow made his way to Leon County.

Henry was a loner. He did not believe in social life and preferred to live in the woods where he didn't have to associate with others on a regular basis. He was about six feet tall, very dark haired, olive skinned and sported a short beard and a handlebar mustache. Most of the time he wore a broad-brimmed black hat and had a pipe in his mouth. He was about the only man in Flo that wore hightopped leather boots that laced up to a point just below his knees. His usual attire was a blue denim coat and surplus olive-drab wool army pants and shirts, beneath which he wore long-handled underwear in both summer and winter. It is said that he would never change his clothes until they literally rotted off him.

Henry was a mountain man in a land of no mountains. He was a hunter, fisherman, trapper and woodcutter by choice and spent most of his life in the woods of the Buffalo Creek bottom and the Trinity River bottom in Leon County. He lived in a shack in the woods and apparently never aspired to anything better. When he needed a few dollars for his necessities, such as tobacco or moonshine whiskey, he would sell the hides of raccoon, o'possum or foxes which he had trapped, or he would sell honey which he robbed from bee trees. He also would sell wood for fireplaces or cookstoves to the residents of the Flo community.

I'll now tell you a true story about Henry, one of dozens that involved him that are repeated to this day in the Flo area. It should give you an idea of his personality.

One Friday evening about dusk, Henry was sitting in his rocking chair on his front porch in the woods near Buffalo Creek. He was facing east, and thinking about what he would do over the weekend. A full moon rose over the timber, which produced a brooding, mystic atmosphere around him, pleasing him very much. He could hear the whip-poor-wills and owls calling to each other across the bottomlands. He thought of a bee tree that he had found the previous spring on the shore of Glaze lake on the Chalacone Ranch, well beyond the town of Oakwood. He had marked the tree with his sign, his initials, using his axe. This tree was located some twenty-five miles almost due north across the woods and swamps from where he sat. He decided to go and rob the bee tree of its honey and decided to do so immediately.

He arose from his chair, walked into the house and picked up a ten-quart bucket, then went outside to the woodpile and picked up his double-bit axe. Looking at the moon for a moment to get his bearings, he then turned and headed north, crosscountry through the woods using the moon as his only guide. As usual, he had no flashlight or lantern to light his way, only the moon. He crossed the branches and creeks where he came to them, not bothering to look for a footlog on which to cross over.

The next morning at first light of day he walked up to the shore of Glaze Lake missing his destination, the bee tree, by only twenty steps.

Henry started to work on the tree immediately, chopping it down and then chopping holes in it to get to the honey the bees had stored inside during the summer. He paid no attention at all to the dozen or so bees that stung him as he was robbing their honey. Taking the sealed honey (bees seal their honey in the comb) he placed it in the ten-quart bucket and headed toward Oakwood, a small town, five miles away through the river bottom.

On his way to Oakwood he came into the small community of St. Paul. By this time he was hungry, so he stopped at a farmer's house and traded a slab of the honey for three biscuits. He had biscuits and honey for breakfast as he walked along.

In the middle of the day he walked into the town of Oakwood, with a population at that time of about five hundred. It was a rough and tough town noted for its fighting men and its illegal moonshine whiskey industry. It had a most unsavory reputation.

Henry located a Negro bootlegger in Oakwood and traded more of his honey for a gallon of moonshine whiskey, which he called "white lightening." He drank some of the whiskey and after an hour or so decided to leave Oakwood and head for home. By now he was feeling no pain of any kind and felt real good. On his way out of town he stopped in front of each house that he came to and gave his blood-curdling Commanche yell. It was said by people who heard it that it could raise the hair on a dead dog. No one bothered Henry Morgan on his way out of town that day.

Henry staggered up to his own porch at three o'clock in the morning on Sunday. He had by now either traded off or eaten all of his honey and had lost the bucket and axe, but he still had a half gallon of the moonshine whiskey left. He sat down in his rocking chair with a huge sigh and thought back over all the things that had happened since he had last sat in the chair at dusk on Friday evening. He considered that the weekend had been entirely successful up to that point and grunted his satisfaction as he rocked back and forth in the chair.

As Henry rocked he would from time to time reach for the moonshine jug that sat by his chair. He was determined to finish off the weekend in style. The weekend and the jug both expired at midnight on Sunday night. Henry always considered it one of the most memorable weekends of his entire life.

Henry died in 1941, but as could have been expected he didn't die from some mere illness, minor or major. He died when a tree fell on him while he was cutting wood.

43

THE BLACK SHEEP

I suppose most families have a burden of some kind to bear. Sometimes it is of a family member that doesn't quite think or operate like the other members, and eventually gets the reputation as the black sheep of the family.

Linsey Rake (not his real name) was the black sheep of one of the Flo families. He died in 1975 after a relatively long life of alternating between being the respectable school teacher that he could be at times and the alcoholic clown that he portrayed at least half of his adult life.

Linsey married a real lady, a beautiful lady, in the early nineteen-thirties. She obviously committed herself to him completely for she stayed with him until her death in 1973. How she managed to do this is a mystery, not only to Linsey's relatives, but to everyone that lived in Flo. Her tombstone, however, does not identify her as a Rake but as her maiden name. Perhaps there is some sort of subtle message there.

Linsey was a foul-mouthed alcoholic, especially in his later years. Alcohol finally killed him. In his wine and roses days he must have done a thousand things, ranging from the slightly amusing, through the bizarre, to the absolutely ridiculous, as a result of his drinking.

Many firmly believe that if he had not become a slave to booze he could have gone far in any endeavor he chose to pursue. He had sufficient brains to be successful. Not many could stand to be around him, however, when he was under the influence of alcohol.

He was a school teacher by profession. From all accounts he was an excellent teacher in the days before drinking began to interfere with his profession.

When he got drunk he would sometimes try to call the President of the United States on the telephone. His purpose was to call the president to try to help him out with some political, domestic or foreign affairs matter that the president didn't seem to understand or be capable of handling. As far as anyone in Flo knows, he never actually talked to the president himself, but he got close to doing so a few times. When he would finally stall out in his efforts to reach him, he would bray like a donkey into the telephone before hanging up. He soon began to call other strangers, as well as his friends and acquaintances, to make his celebrated braying sounds into the telephone.

One of his acquaintances, Miller Lee, had a horse that was prone to kick if you came up too close behind him, especially if you touched him from behind. One day Miller had ridden his horse to Flo and tied the horse near the store. There was a fairly large crowd around. Linsey came by, thoroughly inebriated, and started clowning around near the horse. Miller warned him no less than three times that the horse would kick him if he came too close. Linsey, showing all the bravado the liquor demanded, deliberately walked over behind the horse, grabbed it by the tail, and yanked on it. The horse promptly kicked him halfway through the crowd. Someone must take care of benevolent drunks; he wasn't even bruised.

One day his wife left him at home in an alcoholic glow with a bottle at his elbow and went to church with another lady, who lived nearby. When they returned from church, the neighbor lady let Linsey's wife off at her house and drove on home. Five minutes later she heard the most awful screaming she had ever heard in her entire life coming from Linsey's place. She ran across the road, expecting the worst, thinking the booze had perhaps finally killed Linsey. She found him and his wife fighting each other with garden implements, a hoe and a rake. Linsey was bald as an egg; he had shaved his head while they were at church. When his wife returned home, she found him actually admiring himself in a hand-held mirror in front of a larger mirror. She grabbed the smaller mirror and broke it over his head before they both ran out of the house to arm themselves with the hoe and the rake.

Early one spring, during one of his drinking binges, Linsey took a gill net to Buffalo Creek, a few miles from Flo, and set it out in the creek. A gill net is used to catch fish which try to swim through it and are caught at the gills by the net. The problem was that he abandoned the net, never bothering to go back to the creek to check it for fish or remove it from the water. It is possible that he didn't even remember putting the net in the creek. Late in the spring, Easter Price, a black lady, the matriarch of the entire black population of the Flo area, found five of her goats dead in the creek, each entangled in the gill net Linsey had placed there. He probably never paid her for the goats. She probably never asked for payment. That was the penalty back in those days for being black.

A man named Joe Reddin had a cow that had gotten down and couldn't get up, not an uncommon thing at all. The cow lay there on the ground in the hot sun a week. Linsey stumbled across her one day and told Joe about her. Joe told him that if he dragged her into the shade and she lived he could have her. Linsey tied her to his truck and dragged her to the nearest shade about two hundred yards away. When he got her there he discovered that all the hair had been scraped from the cow on the side that was on the ground. When he took the rope off she immediately stood on her feet and started grazing. He quit drinking for two full days after that.

Linsey taught school over the years, not only in Flo but over an area perhaps a hundred miles or so in various directions from Flo. He became the principal at several of the schools. After he moved on from one of the schools, they discovered that he had sawed a hole in the floor under his desk so that he would have a place to hide his whiskey.

No one in Flo ever hated Linsey for very long. He will be remembered and talked about there for at least another hundred years.

IV - THE LATER YEARS (1941-1993)

44

THE CROSSCUT SAW

During World War II, many of the Flo men either went into the military service or moved to cities like Houston to work in the shipyards where money was to be made. That left a dearth of able-bodied men in Flo and it was common for neighbors to trade work on jobs that required two or more men to accomplish.

Bud Smith was a farmer that lived in Flo before and after the war. He was a serious minded old fellow that sometimes stuttered when he talked, especially if he got excited.

Bud was working with Woodrow Bell cutting wood for their fireplaces and wood cook stoves, which were the only means of heat available in Flo back then. Bud had a good quality crosscut saw, about six feet long, that required a man on each end of it to operate. Over a period of several days it became more and more dull and finally got to the point where it was wearing them out trying to pull it through the oak hardwood they were cutting.

"We've got to get this saw sharpened," said Woodrow. "It's killing me."

"I agree," said Bud, "I-I-I'll take it tomorrow to Walker Moore and have-have-have him sharpen it for us."

The following morning about sunup Bud passed Evan Moore's place, which was on the way to Walker's place, where he was taking the saw to get it sharpened. He visited with Evan, as was the Flo custom, for a few minutes before resuming his journey.

He soon arrived at Walker's place and tried to leave the saw and return home, where other work was waiting to be done. Walker objected, however, because he wanted someone to talk to for a few hours.

"You can't leave," said Walker, "because you have to hold the saw while I sharpen it." Bud didn't really know whether this statement was a lie or not (it was) so he stayed and held the saw.

Sharpening a crosscut saw is not a simple task, such as sharpening a knife, but requires specialized knowledge and special skills. The special skills involve the use of a certain type file for sharpening each cutting tooth on the saw, use of a mechanical device in conjunction with a ball-peen hammer to produce the "set" in each tooth, and still another file to produce the edge on the drag teeth, which clean out the slot in the wood after the cutting teeth have made their cut. If one does not do all these things carefully and skillfully, the saw can later cause all kinds of problems to the users.

It took Walker all day long to sharpen Bud's saw. Normally, it would have taken him only about two hours, but he had a captive audience here and he took full advantage of it. He would make a pass with the file on one of the saw's teeth (there were literally dozens of them), then stop and talk to Bud for a few minutes before making the next move.

Bud sat and sweated, fumed and fussed silently all day long. He didn't dare say anything critical to Walker about the delay because he was afraid Walker would stop work on the saw then and there. He knew there was only one thing worse than a dull saw and that was a saw that was sharp on one end and dull on the other. The only other saw sharpener that he knew lived clear across the county. He just gritted his teeth and waited.

Just as the sun was setting, Bud passed Evan's place on his way home with the saw. He had a terrible frown on his face and was taking steps about nine feet long. Evan spoke to him, expecting him to visit for a few minutes. Bud just grunted at him and kept right on walking.

A couple of weeks later the saw had gotten dull again. Woodrow and Bud were each down on one knee wearing themselves out trying to cut wood with it.

"You've got to go back and get Walker to sharpen your saw again," said Woodrow.

"Why-Why-Why I wouldn't go back to that old son-of-a-bitch *for* a crosscut saw!" said Bud.

45

LEROY WILSON'S BRAND

There was a fellow named Leroy Wilson, who lived in or near Centerville, the county seat of Leon County, some years ago. He was a big, burly man with a heavy beard, brusque voice and a no-nonsense attitude toward life and his fellow man. When he had a job to do he went at it without stopping to consider whether there might be an easier and perhaps more efficient way to do it.

Leroy bought a small herd of cows one time and put them in one of his pastures. Pretty soon he discovered that one of his cows was missing. This was not an uncommon occurrence in those days because most of the fences were broken-down, rusty relics of their former selves. Even new fences won't stand up long in Leon County without constant maintenance, because trees are always falling on them and knocking them flat.

Upon discovering that his cow was missing, Leroy spent several days repairing the fences around his pasture. He then went cow hunting, searching the area for miles around. He failed to find his cow and he could not find anyone in the area who had even seen his cow.

One day, during the search, he rode out of the brush into one of the one- lane, unpaved county roads and met another fellow on horseback, named Wade Parks, who was driving a herd of steers down the dirt road. Wade Parks had a way with livestock. The steers were calm and peaceful and continued to stay in the road, even though there were no fences alongside the road.

"How the hell do you manage to drive these steers down this unfenced road, through this brush without having them all run away?" asked the thoroughly exasperated Leroy.

Wade, a small, thinking type of fellow, puffed on his pipe and looked at Leroy, who had lost his hat in the brush, was bleeding from several brush scratches, had his clothes half torn off him, and whose horse was winded and completely wet with sweat. After a while Wade said, "Well, first of all, Leroy, you've got to have more common sense than the damned cows you're driving." Wade and Leroy were never very close friends after this conversation between them.

After about two months Leroy gave up the search for his cow, but continued his grumbling about cow thieves that he felt certain had stolen her.

One day, some three months after the cow had disappeared, Leroy almost ran into her with his truck on one of the dirt roads near his pasture. He jumped out of the truck, grabbed his lariat, roped the cow and tied her to a tree. He then built a fire beside the road, heated a running iron in the fire until it was white hot, and proceeded to burn his full name, "LEROY WILSON", in capital letters on the cow's right side, starting near her rump and extending across her body to her shoulder.

Leroy tied the cow to his truck and more or less dragged her to his pasture where he released her. He kicked her in the rump as he let her go and yelled, "Now damn you, if you run away again, I'll burn 'CENTERVILLE, TEXAS' across your other side!"

The cow must have understood Leroy's threat because she never disappeared from his pasture again.

46

THE TRAINING OF OL' JACK

If I should live long enough to forget all my childhood memories, the last that would fade away would be the memory of my father's attempts to train our gray-nosed mule to stop doing certain things that the fool mule insisted on doing.

This mule--we called him "Ol' Jack"--was not all that unique from a physical standpoint, weighing perhaps a thousand pounds, coal black except for his nose, spindly legged and slightly humped in the back. His nose was gray and looked as if he had plunged it into a bucket of wet cement halfway to his eyes and then let it dry until it was the color of ancient concrete. Ol' Jack was slow, both mentally and physically. I remember learning to plow our crops with him when I was eleven years old.

I was just a youngster in 1935 when I saw the first encounter between my old man and Ol' Jack. It was a Sunday afternoon in East Texas in July, so hot eggs could be fried on a sidewalk, had a sidewalk been available. The temperature and humidity were so high we boys and my old man were lying about, naked above the waist and barefooted, in the breezeway that ran completely through our ramshackle farm house from north to south. We had straight-backed chairs turned upside-down on the floor and lay in a semi-upright position with our bare backs against the cross pieces in the chairs with pillows under our heads. Sweat was running off our bodies onto the pillows and chairs and forming puddles on the wooden floor beneath us. We were not only praying for a breeze, a breeze of any size, but were also keeping a keen eye on the absolutely cloudless sky, hoping that a thunderhead would poke its nose above the horizon to the west.

I'm telling you all this so that you will understand just how hot, slow, bored, frustrated and tired we all were just waiting for some sort of *change* to occur. A hound chasing a chicken from underneath the house, which was set on blocks above the ground such that you could easily crawl under it, would have made our day. The problem was, the hounds and chickens were just as bored and hot as we were and were hoping *we* would start something exciting.

"Look at that fool mule," my old man said from his position on his upside-down chair. "He's gonna eat up to the fence and when he gits there he's gonna eat over it as an excuse to lean on the wire and scratch his chest."

Nobody answered him. After all, he hadn't asked a direct question and we weren't in the mood for just chitchat. Waving at the gnats was exhausting enough. We watched in silence as Ol' Jack grazed up to the fence, about sixty yards across the pasture from where we lay. The only sound we could hear was the high-pitched whine of cicadas, which we called "dry flies," screaming to the world about how hot and humid it was out there.

Ol' Jack must have been asleep or nearly so, his grazing merely a reflex action, because we saw him graze right into the three-wire, barbed-wire fence. When he hit it he jerked his head up and snapped his big ears forward to see what he had blundered into. Recognizing the fence, he raised his head and neck high and lumbered forward, pressing his chest against the wires.

He shuffled his body back and forth on the wires until he was comfortable then stretched his head forward and downward to graze on the opposite side. He used the fence to support most of his weight, a comfortable position for a mule, but not at all good for the fence which threatened to collapse at any moment.

"Fetch me my pump gun," the old man said out of the corner of his mouth in my direction. "I'm gonna train this fool mule not to eat over my fences."

We all snapped to attention. Here was action beyond our wildest dreams. I skittered into the house and brought out the .20-gauge pump gun, already loaded with high-powered shells of number six shot--"squirrel shot" we called it.

The old man didn't even sit up straight. He merely raised his knees, laid the gun across them and turned them ever so slightly to line up the sights on the rear end of the mule. All our eyes turned to the mule, waiting expectantly.

The explosion was deafening, the blast bounding off the walls of the breezeway we were in and ringing our ears for at least an hour. No one even noticed. We were all fascinated by the action at the fence.

I can still see it in slow motion. First a cloud of dust popped two feet into the air in every direction away from the rump of Ol' Jack. A terrible noise, like a clap of thunder but more like a giant piece of new canvas being torn apart by great unseen hands came from the mule. A blue haze rose slowly from the mule's rear, slowly dissipating into the hot, simmering air. Simultaneously, Ol' Jack tried to turn himself inside out by shoving his rear end through his chest. Since this was impossible, his whole body catapulted forward like a cannonball from a cannon. The fence was torn down for twenty-five yards on each side of him. The wires ended up looped across the mule's chest. He raced forward, braying like his jackass father, dragging wire and broken fence posts out into the road that paralleled the fence. He ran to the top of the hill, a hundred yards away, before he stopped in the road and looked back, his head high on his up-stretched neck with his long donkey ears switching alternately and then in unison forward and backward, while he stood and snorted, rolling his eyes, searching desperately for whatever it was that had attacked him.

I won't even try to explain our reaction to what we had seen, other than to say that I have never come so near death, before or since; death from lack of oxygen, caused from laughing so hard that I couldn't get my breath. Finally I collapsed, falling off the front porch and turning an ankle in the process.

One would think that this little episode would have been enough to teach Ol' Jack not to eat over any more fences. Not so. I suspect that some internal urge that he was not capable of resisting *forced* him to continue eating over fences.

Ol' Jack did, however, develop a defense mechanism against being shot by the old man after he finally discovered that the old man was the cause of his troubles. Many times afterward I would see him graze into a fence, always acting surprised when he hit it. Then, before eating over it, he would turn his back to it and survey the area all around for several minutes, looking for the old man and his dreaded shotgun. If the old man was nowhere to be seen, he would eventually turn around and eat over the fence, but would raise his head from time to time to survey the area, just in case.

The mule's new-found caution was not always successful, for the old man began a campaign, to the delight of us boys, to outwit Ol' Jack. When the mule grazed into the fence then turned to survey the area, the old man would hide until the mule finally decided it was safe and proceeded to stretch his neck over the fence. The old man would then take the shotgun, and slipping from tree to tree, or from any object that would provide cover to the next, would eventually get within range and blast away. One time he even had me drive his pickup truck slowly past the mule, with him lying hidden in the back, so that he could get his shot. Ol' Jack never failed to tear down from ten to fifty feet of fence, which I was required to repair. It was a labor of love, however, for I couldn't wait to get it repaired so we could wait for the next incident.

I noticed, after a while, that if no fence was near when Ol' Jack heard an explosion, he would run until he found a fence, and *then* he would tear it down. I believe he thought that was what was expected of him. Over the years he tore down a lot of fences as a result of hearing a loud clap of thunder from a passing thunderstorm. In a sense, I suppose, my old man *had* trained this fool mule--to tear down a fence, whether near or far, when he heard an explosion.

I still remember the last contest that I witnessed between the old man and Ol' Jack. It occurred about a week before I left home to face the world, at seventeen years of age, in January 1941. It was a Saturday morning and the old man had been inside the house all morning. The mule apparently thought he had gone to town, as he almost always did on Saturday mornings. Ol' Jack, half asleep as usual, grazed into a fence near the house. After doing his customary inspection of the surrounding area, he proceeded to enjoy his favorite pastime, leaning on a fence while eating over it. The old man saw the mule at the fence through the window. He got his shotgun and from deep inside the house, well out of sight, shot Ol' Jack in the rump. The problem was that he forgot to raise the window and the family spent the next two years with cardboard in the window instead of glass. The usual results occurred where the mule was standing. There was a pall of dust, a great ripping sound, and a blue haze. Fifty feet of wire and fence posts disappeared up the road, draped across the chest of Ol' Jack.

Now that I look back on this contest, after all these years, with perfect hindsight of course, I realize that the things that happened were funny to everyone involved except Ol' Jack. To make matters a great deal worse, however, is to remember how Ol' Jack died. When he grew old, my old man turned him out, in the middle of the winter, onto the county road that ran through Flo past our farm. He never bothered to feed the old mule at all so he grew very emaciated (the locals called it "pore") and finally lay down near our farm and could not get up. The old man decided, and rightly so, that the mule had to be destroyed.

Back in those days one didn't call a veterinarian to destroy an animal that was on its last legs. The old man took his shotgun, loaded with buckshot, and went to Ol' Jack to put him out of his misery. Instead of shooting him in the head from close range, he backed off about twenty yards or so and shot him in the chest. I believe he wanted to see what a load of buckshot would do to a thousand pound animal from that distance. The only other animal that was hunted with a shotgun and buckshot back in those days was white-tailed deer that weighed up to 150 pounds.

Ol' Jack didn't die instantly upon being shot. Instead, he turned his head toward the old man and brayed at him long and loud for perhaps ten seconds before he died.

The sound of Ol' Jack braying at him haunted my old man all the rest of his life. He broke down and cried when he told me about it several years later. He always thought that it was Ol' Jack's way of getting even with him for abusing him with the shotgun all those years and especially for the fact that he had allowed him to nearly starve to death after the mule had worked for him and the family for about twenty-five years.

47

JOE BELL' S OLD SOW

I took a break in my studies at the University of Colorado after the spring semester in 1948 and came to Texas with my wife and baby daughter to spend a month or two. That was a big mistake because it was summer and we were in no way prepared to face the heat and humidity offered by Leon County. We stayed with my parents in Flo for a month, before we decided we either had to leave for Colorado soon or die.

During the month we were in Flo, I had no choice but to get involved with the things my father was doing at the time. You either got involved or had to leave. I was not treated as a guest, with guest privileges, by any stretch of the imagination. I ended up working like a dog, as I remember, on the crops and doing other things like repairing fences in the one hundred degree heat and eighty percent humidity.

One reason we were repairing fences was because my father was raising a corn crop on one of our places, a sand hill farm about five miles southwest of the Flo crossroads. One of Joe Bell's sows and a couple of her shoats were getting into the cornfield and eating our corn. We were repairing holes in the net wire fence that was supposed to protect the corn crop from hogs.

One day about noon we went to the cornfield and the old man took his shotgun with him and gave one to me. When we got there, he told me to walk along the fence line on one side of the field and he would walk along the fence line on the other side looking for holes in the fence that Joe's hogs were using. His specific instruction to me was to kill any of Joe's hogs that I might run across on my inspection of the fence. We were to eventually meet along the fence line at the back of the field.

I remember walking along the edge of the corn in the heat, looking at the fence, while sweating like a pig and wishing to hell I was back in colorful Colorado breathing that cool mountain air.

Suddenly, I was snapped out of my reverie by a loud WHUFF! WHUFF! coming from some small bushes next to the cornfield. I looked in that direction and saw Joe's old sow trying to sneak away through the brush and grass. I threw up the shotgun and lined up the sights on her shoulder. It would have been an easy kill.

All of a sudden I thought about Joe Bell, the owner of the hog. Joe and his friend, Marquis Taylor, had been my not-so-secret heroes ever since I had been a youngster. I don't know of anything that they ever did that would have caused anyone, even a kid, to think of them as heroes, but small boys sometimes pick out an older boy to worship, even though the older boy may very well be more outlaw than Sir Galahad. This was the case here.

In any event, I couldn't pull the trigger. I stood there and watched the sow head for the fence at a trot and go through a hole under the wire.

Ten minutes later I met my father at the back of the field and told him about seeing the sow. He demanded an explanation why I had not shot at her, and eyed me with suspicion when I told him that she was out of range when I spotted her. To have told him that I didn't have the heart to kill Joe Bell's sow would have been downright dangerous at the time.

We repaired the fence in about ten minutes and headed for a neighbor's house about a mile away. The neighbor's name was Claude Mullins and he had some good hog dogs. He agreed to go with us back to the cornfield and have his dogs bay the old sow. I don't know to this day what the old man planned to do with the sow once the dogs bayed her, but I fully believe he expected to kill her on the spot, even though he was at the time and had always been Joe's friend, having helped Joe out from time to time when Joe was a young man.

We went back to the cornfield and Claude's dogs picked up the sow's trail right away and the race was on. She ran all over the countryside sticking to the brush, creeks, bogs and thickets. Finally, after about thirty minutes, the dogs bayed her about a half mile or so from the cornfield. When we got there we found her in the bottom of a narrow, steep-sided creek bed, in the water, apparently dead from heat exhaustion.

While we were standing around talking, the old man looked over at Claude and saw that he was very pale and was gasping for breath. He thought Claude was about to die from a stroke, heart attack, or heat exhaustion because of the temperature and humidity, and the fact that we had been chasing through the brush trying to keep up with the hog and the dogs. He had Claude lie down on the ground for a while before we finally left the hog and went back to the truck.

We dropped Claude and his dogs off at his house and drove over to where Joe lived a mile or so away to tell him the bad news about his sow.

As we approached Joe's house, the old man removed a P38 semi-automatic pistol, made in a foreign country, from under the seat in the truck and placed it on the seat beside him. He covered it with a piece of paper so that it could not be seen from outside the truck.

"What the hell are you doing?" I asked. I didn't care too much about the idea of approaching my boyhood hero with a concealed weapon.

"Joe's a friend of mine," said the old man. "Always has been and always will be. I wouldn't think of hurting him in any way, but if he goes nuts when I tell him his old sow is dead, I don't plan to die at his hands because he is in a rage over a damn hog."

Joe was home and came out to the truck when we drove up. When the old man told him about his hog dying and how she died, he took it very well indeed and didn't even raise his voice in protest, although I could tell that he wasn't at all happy about it. The old man told him where he could find her (Joe knows every nook and cranny of all the woods in the Flo area even to this day), but I believe that he never bothered to go get her.

Joe never knew that the old man had the pistol handy in case he had to use it, and will be surprised if he ever reads this story and learns about it.

As for pale and gasping Claude Mullins, he lived to be almost one hundred years old, dying around 1990 I believe. He only outlived my father, who died in 1954, by about thirty six years.

Joe Bell, now more than eighty years old, is ailing some, but being my boyhood hero I keep urging him to hang in there so that he can see the new century roll around.

48

HOG STEALER

In the nineteen-thirties we had what was referred to as open range in Leon County in general and in the Flo community and surrounding areas specifically. Open range meant that one did not have to keep his livestock enclosed in a fenced area, but was allowed to let them roam freely over the countryside with everyone else's stock. If you raised a crop, or even a garden, you were responsible for fencing the livestock out of your property, rather than fencing your own livestock in on your property.

The open range law caused all kinds of problems for at least a hundred and fifty years before 1950, when enough property in the area had been fenced to make the system obsolete.

I would estimate that approximately one-third of all the men in the area had livestock in the woods. Since the livestock were all mixed together, each man would ride the woods at least one day each week to locate, doctor, brand, and mark his own stock and, when ready, round up his stock for selling on the market, either at an auction sale in Buffalo or at the stockyards in Fort Worth.

While in the woods, the stock hunters were usually on a horse with a hunting horn, lariat and rifle on his saddle, and with two or more stock dogs (which the locals called "hog" dogs) with him. The dogs would locate the stock (especially the hogs) and "bay" them. The hunter would then ride to his barking dogs. Many times he would discover that his dogs had bayed someone else's hogs or stock and he would ride on, blowing his hunting horn to call his dogs away from the stock they had found and bayed.

As a boy in the nineteen-thirties, I remember hearing as many as four different hunters in the woods, simultaneously looking for their stock. Many times a single group of hogs would be bayed four different times by four different sets of dogs.

It was inevitable that under such conditions there had to be at least a man or two in the area that would get a little careless about whose hogs or pigs or cattle he rounded up for market, especially the stock that were not specifically branded or marked. Sooner or later, of course, such a man would be suspected of being a hog, cow or horse stealer, but even if he was caught in the act he could usually manage some sort of excuse for his actions (after all, almost all the stockmen were kin to each other to some degree) and would not end up hanging from a tree or in jail for his sins.

When I visited Flo in the spring of 1992, I was talking to an old friend about the open range law and he told me the following true story. Since all the men in the story are still alive and well, I have had to use fictitious names for them.

"My wife and I lived about five miles from the Flo crossroads on a farm," my old friend Jess Davis told me. "Two old sows and a half dozen half-grown shoats showed up at our place in the woods one day and I noticed that they weren't marked. I went to the Flo store and put out the word that they were around my place and that the owner had better come and get them right away, because if they got through my fences into my crops I was going to kill them all.

"Two days later, about noon, old Bill Leyland came riding up to my place from out of the woods on a broken-down horse, along with two hog dogs that were trailing him. Old Bill had been an open range stock man all his life and has always had hogs and cows, especially hogs, in the woods. From time to time people suspected him of stealing stock, but nothing ever came of it and I had no reason to believe that he could be a stock thief.

"Bill had me describe the two sows and shoats I had been seeing and immediately stated that they were his hogs and that he was there to pen them and take them to Fort Worth and sell them. He asked me if I knew where they were and I told him they were on a creek about two hundred yards from my house. He asked me if I would help him put them in a pen near my barn and I agreed to do so.

"We went to the creek and his dogs bayed the hogs immediately. It took us about thirty minutes to move the hogs to my place and get them into the pen. One thing I'll say for Bill. He had two good hog dogs and he and the dogs knew how to handle hogs.

"After the hogs were penned, Bill told me that he was going to ride back to his house and get his pickup truck and come back to get the hogs. As he mounted his horse to leave, and old, gray-haired Negro man, named Justin Price, walked up to my yard. He lived at a Negro settlement called Pleasant Spring five miles away.

"'Hello, Mr. Bill and Mr. Jess,' said Justice. 'I've come lookin' for my hogs that have been missing for a week. There are two ol' sows and six half-grown shoats with them. Some white folks back down the road a piece said they saw them a couple of days ago. Have you seen them?' He eyed Bill on his horse and his two hog dogs.

"Bill looked at me," said Jess, "with this strange expression on his face and without hesitation turned back to Justice and said, 'Yeah, I just got through penning them for you. I was about to come tell you where they were. I believe you owe me one of them shoats for penning them for you, don't you?'

"'Well, Mister Bill, that sounds fair to me,' said Justice after a moment.

"I didn't have the courage to tell Justice that Bill was in the process of stealing his hogs, using me as an accomplice, and that he had arrived just in time to save all of them except the one Bill had asked for.

"Justice took his remaining hogs home, walking and herding them with a stick," said Jess. "Bill returned to my place in his truck and picked up the shoat that he had essentially purloined from Justice. To this day Bill has never said a single word to me about his actions that day."

49

OL' BLUE

Evan Moore, finished with the job of installing a glass panel in one of the four small window frames in the back door of his ranch house, began putting his tools back into his tool box.

"That ought to last at least fifty years," he said to his wife, Opal. "They were out of regular glass at the lumber yard, so they sold me a pane of tempered glass instead. I doubt if you could break it with a hammer."

"Ol' Blue has used that hole in the door all summer for getting into and out of the house," Opal said, referring to their house cat. "He's going to be disappointed when he has to scratch on the door for us to let him in and out."

"Can't be helped," said Evan. "Winter is coming. He'll get used to it."

An hour later, Opal saw Ol' Blue emerge from the woods that came up to their back yard and start his patented strut across the open yard. He was a medium-sized tom with snow white hair (a name like Ol' White or Ol' Snow would have been more fitting than Ol' Blue), a perfectly round face, and crossed green eyes that looked out upon the world as if he owned it. He moved across the ground with a pompous bearing, at least as haughty as the Pope entering St. Peter's Basilica. Opal subconsciously looked for the royal escort of bands, honor guard, emissaries, servants and perhaps even a harem that should have accompanied such a dignitary as this. One thing only spoiled the scene; Ol' Blue's tail had been bobbed two inches from his rump.

He was not a Manx, a natural bobtail, therefore he had to have lost the tail in some sort of accident. Even Opal, had she have been able to converse with him, would never have brought up the subject of the bobbed tail. It just wouldn't have seemed right to talk about it.

Ol' Blue walked slowly and deliberately--arrogantly is a more descriptive word--between Evan's stock dogs, Rye and Shag, who were lying twenty feet apart in the shade of a giant oak tree that grew in the yard. He split the distance between them perfectly. He disdained their very presence, a prince walking between two resting slaves, looking at neither as he made his way toward the back door of the house.

The dogs watched him in despair, their blood seething. He might as well have been a small, effeminate, male hairdresser, with curly golden locks, dressed in a satin shirt and velvet pants, mincing across the floor of a cowboy bar in some place like Lordsburg, New Mexico or Chugwater, Wyoming. Ol' Blue was asking for it. When he was halfway between the dogs and the back door, his nose in the air as usual, Rye and Shag could stand it no longer. Both simultaneously bellowed in rage as they leaped to their feet and charged him with serious mutilation in their hearts.

Ol' Blue let them cover half the distance to him before he abandoned his class act and reacted, sprinting for his life for the safety of the back door.

Opal watched it all. She later said that Ol' Blue was running so fast that he looked like a white shoestring, a pale streak zipping through the air, rarely if ever touching the ground. Rye and Shag, singing their stock dog song, kicked up gravel and grass for yards in their desperate attempt to come up to his speed. As the cat crossed the porch and the dogs tore splinters out of the porch steps trying to catch him, Opal remembered the new pane of glass Evan had recently installed in the door.

"No, Blue! No! No!" she screamed. Too late. He had already launched himself from the porch in a long smooth glide, a meteor in flight, arcing like an arrow for the center of the target with satisfaction in his soul and a look of smugness on his face.

He hit the tempered plate glass at full speed, nose first. He may as well have hit a brick wall. As his brain was jarred and the bright light of day snapped off, his body, which kept on coming even though his head was at a standstill against the glass, began to envelope his head. A split second later the metamorphosis had been completed. He was no longer cat shaped. He looked more like a giant frying pan with the lid on, covered by fine white fur. It differed from the shape of a frying pan primarily by the fact that it had not one but four handles distributed helter-skelter around the periphery, each one consisting of a cat's leg, sticking straight out, claws bared.

The two dogs that had planned a few seconds earlier to tear the cat to pieces if only they could catch him, threw on their brakes as soon as he accordioned himself against the door. Their paws, however, were not designed for quick stops on wooden floors so they slid face first into the lower part of the door, just as Ol' Blue slid in slow motion down the door toward the floor. The dogs panicked when they saw the fur covered apparition falling on them from above, and almost ruptured themselves getting off the porch so that they could study this phenomenon from a safe distance, barking at it all the while.

Opal rushed to the door, picked up poor Ol' Blue by the claw-ended legs, opened the door and took him inside, talking baby talk to him. She was wasting her breath. He didn't regain consciousness for two hours and couldn't hear a thing for several days.

Ol' Blue lay on his belly in the short grass, his head low, his lower jaw lying on the ground, sizing up his victim.

Evan watched the cat stalk the squirrel. Ol' Blue's a joke, he thought. He thinks the squirrel can't see him while, in fact, he stands out like a neon sign with his snow white fur and bright green eyes, especially since he's lying on his belly in the middle of a freshly mowed lawn without any cover whatever to hide him. He's even going through the motions of hypnotizing the squirrel by switching his tail like the big hunting cats do. The problem is, he's bobtailed.

The squirrel moved closer, aware of the cat but not overly concerned. His species hadn't managed to survive all these millions of years without knowing a few things about avoiding predators.

Suddenly, Ol' Blue charged. He kept low and moved at great speed, his claws tearing at the roots of the grass as he accelerated. The squirrel broke for the tree before the cat's claws had left the ground on his first jump. Ol' Blue rapidly closed the gap between them. The squirrel hit the tree trunk two feet above the ground. The cat hit the tree at the same spot a split second later, but the squirrel was no longer there, having scooted around the tree to the other side. They both climbed the tree as fast as they could, the squirrel perhaps a foot ahead of the cat. The squirrel was climbing for his life now, totally surprised at the ferocity of the cat's pursuit and his climbing ability. The squirrel climbed higher and higher into smaller and smaller branches of the tree, the cat on his tail. Finally, the squirrel went out on the topmost limb which bent under his weight. He expected Ol' Blue to give up the chase here, but the cat kept right on coming. The squirrel was left with no choice; he bailed out of the tree, spreading his legs and tail wide as he sailed through the air from fifteen feet up, landing on the ground and scampering away to the next larger tree.

While the squirrel was in his free fall, reality came back to Ol' Blue. Up until then he thought he had it made, but suddenly he realized that he weighed six times as much as the squirrel and that he had, for the last few seconds been climbing small limbs, twigs really, that didn't have a prayer of supporting his weight. He considered bailing out of the tree as the squirrel had done, but after one squint at the ground decided against it. After all, he was not all rawhide and muscle like the squirrel and even though he knew he would land on his feet, nothing would keep his soft belly from smacking the ground.

Evan watched the cat climb right out of the top of the tree even though he was trying to stop, grab at the sky then turn a somersault as he headed back for the tree with all four legs outstretched, talons exposed to grab *anything* on the tree that would break his fall. He landed a third of the way down the tree, but at the end of small branches which wouldn't support his weight. His legs turned to blurs as his claws fought the air trying to find something solid to latch onto. No such luck. He merely fell further down the side of the tree into more limbs that wouldn't support his weight, where he repeated the flurry of activity again trying to gain a foothold.

Evan watched him go through this process twice more before he finally fell belly up from the ends of the lowest branches of the tree a few feet above the ground. To his surprise, Ol' Blue didn't bother to twist his body and land on his feet. He appeared to have given up completely, as if he was thinking to hell with it. As a consequence he fell flat on his back, feet up. He lay in that position until Evan came over and reached down for him.

He snarled and hissed at Evan, rolled over, got up and walked slowly and majestically toward the house just as if he had been named Grand Overall Champion of the International Feline Exposition at some fabulous hotel on the French Riviera. Evan couldn't help but notice that he limped a little. He never laughed aloud at Ol' Blue, however. You don't laugh at someone that you *know* is embarrassed to death and is trying desperately to not let it show.

It was a bad day in Leon County, Texas. The rain clouds hung down at two-hundred feet. Rumbles of thunder marched inexorably north to south across the scrub oak and pine woods. Opal went around her house closing the windows. As she started to close the one that faced her back yard, she saw Ol' Blue sitting on top of the head of the concrete maiden that stood atop the concrete double shells that in turn were balanced on top of the concrete pedestal that sat on the ground next to the blue Fiberglas fishpond. Water flowed from an urn held in the maiden's hands into the top small shell then into the larger shell then into the fishpond. The cat looked like a concrete statue on top of the maiden's head except that he was snow white instead of concrete gray. If he had been blessed with a long tail it would no doubt have been curled across in front of his body just above his front feet. He sat motionless, not even moving his eyes.

"Get your fanny in here!" Opal called to him. "You're going to get soaking wet out there." He didn't bother to turn his head to look at her. He was practicing his Buddha role; no earthly thing could possibly warrant his attention.

As Opal closed the last window, she saw the lightning flashes and heard thunder boom around the house. Ol' Blue was still sitting on top of the maiden's head, disdainful of the weather, arrogant as one of the old Gods. Just as she reached for the window again, intending to raise it to speak firmly to the cat, she saw a streak of lightning hit Ol' Blue from above and simultaneously heard a mighty crash of thunder which shook the entire house. Although bits of concrete fountain flew in every direction, she ignored it for she was watching Ol' Blue leap four feet into the air and assume the rigid position of the cat you see on doors and windows of houses on Halloween night. You know the picture--big hump in the back, every hair standing out from the body, four legs and tail extended straight out, claws bared, teeth exposed, snarl on the face and the entire body stiff as wire. He performed a double somersault in the air and fell, feet first, into the fishpond below.

"My God! Evan!" she screamed to her husband who was reading the newspaper in another room. "Ol' Blue's been struck by lightning at the fishpond. He's in the water. Go get him, quick!"

Evan ambled out into the yard, thinking about the nine lives a cat is supposed to have and remembering that he had only one. He was not all that anxious to grab a wire-haired cat out of a pond at the place a lightning bolt had hit only a few moments earlier.

When he finally arrived at the pond he saw the cat, as rigid as the concrete of the fountain, standing still-legged in the pond, water halfway up his sides and covering his head. He reached down and grabbed him by his stub tail and lifted his frazzled body out of the pond. The cat didn't make a move of any kind. Evan didn't bother to examine him; he was obviously graveyard dead. He carried his body across the yard and threw him in the garbage can and closed the lid firmly over him.

Two days later, Ralph Taylor, the son of one of the Moore's neighbors, drove up to the garbage cans and began to dump them into his father's pickup truck, his monthly task for which he was paid four dollars by the Moores. When he removed the lid from the fifth garbage can, he got the scare of his sixteen-year life. A screaming, squalling, dirty-white banshee with razor sharp claws came roaring out of the can trying to rip him to pieces, drawing blood from his hand immediately and shredding his sleeve clear to his shoulder as it proceeded to climb him. As Ol' Blue passed his face he ripped his ear and split his nose, finally trashing the sloppy cap he wore before he jumped on top of the pickup, then into the lower branches of the tree under which the truck was parked. He disappeared high into the branches of the tree.

A profound silence descended over the yard except for the steady, methodical cursing of Ralph.

213

Never again would he nonchalantly rip off the lid of a garbage can, but would lean way back as he very slowly eased up the lid to look inside.

Opal stepped back from the Christmas tree that she had just completed decorating, admiring the result of her four hours of work. She had finally talked Evan into cutting the tree for her and setting it up in the living room in its three-prong metal stand, even strung two sets of Christmas lights on it. After that he had managed to get lost. It was just as well--she loved to decorate the tree alone when she could take all the time she needed to do the job to her complete satisfaction. First she flocked it in white, then added some fifty decorations. On the very top she added her favorite ornament, a lighted angel with a halo, tilted head, mouth open in silent song. She stepped back and admired the large tree which went clear to the ceiling. It was beautiful.

Opal gathered up all the cardboard boxes that had contained the Christmas decorations and took them outside to store on the back porch until after the holidays. Since it was a warm day in Leon County, she left the back door open while she stored the boxes. When she started back toward the door she saw Ol' Blue start his ridiculous, mincing swagger across the back yard toward the house. He was really putting on a show for the two stock dogs, Rye and Shag, who watched him, fascinated, from their positions in the yard.

The cat had seen Opal leave the back door open, so safety was at hand as soon as he entered the house, so he thought. Knowing that he could outrun the dogs to the back door, he began his strut, just rubbing it in.

Both dogs exploded from their positions simultaneously, bellowing as loud as they could, ripping furrows in the grass in their attempt to get started. Their legs were blurs under them as they tried to accelerate. To Opal it looked like they had actually jumped into the air to get their legs going at the maximum rate before they came down to where their claws could rip the grass to shreds. By this time Ol' Blue, with a self-satisfied look on his face, was stretched out like a greyhound racing for the back door. Opal also raced for the door. The cat entered the house first, the two dogs on his tail. As Opal arrived in the doorway she saw Ol' Blue disappear under the Christmas tree in the living room and saw the two dogs, although desperately trying to stop, slide into the bottom of the tree. The next thing she saw was an oscillation of branches, decorations, lights and silver icicles move up the tree from bottom to top. As it arrived at the top of the tree she saw the cat's round, cross-eyed face pop out from under the decorations, his head against the ceiling, his front legs encircling the lighted angel who apparently didn't realize what was going on for she continued her silent song without even a change of expression. By this time, decorations of every size and description, along with bark and needles from the tree were falling in showers toward the floor. Both dogs were scrabbling at the floor trying to get out from under the falling debris.

Opal watched the tree slowly tip over and fall to the floor. There was a great crash of decorations, lights, silver icicles, lighted angel, tree limbs and one cross-eyed cat. As the tree fell, Opal looked into the face of Ol' Blue as he went past, still clinging tightly to the fallen angel. His crossed eyes were reproachful, begging her forgiveness, but imploring her to blame the damn dogs who were the cause of the problem in the first place.

"Get out of here!" Opal screamed.

When the tree hit the floor the two dogs and the cat simultaneously bolted for the door, going out together at full speed, their antagonism toward each other completely forgotten in the face of this far greater threat to life and limb.

Opal breathed deeply and grabbed the tree just below the angel and started raising it, moving down the tree with her hands as she slowly raised it to an upright position. The stand it was in was still firmly attached to it. She stood back and looked it over. It was a complete disaster.

At that precise moment, Evan, who had missed all the action, walked through the front door. He looked at the tree for a few seconds then turned to Opal.

"It looks great, honey," he said, feeling guilty and trying to make amends for being absent and not helping her with the decorations. "How did you manage to decorate it so beautifully this year?"

50

TOM BILL FEATHERSTON
LIVED HARD, DIED YOUNG

In the summer of 1949, Ben Lee was the sheriff of Leon County. He served a total of fifteen years. He had been elected in 1947 for two primary reasons. One was that he came from a family of well respected, big, rugged men who always faced their problems and obligations with integrity and courage. Another reason was because Leon County had, since the end of World War II, approached a state of anarchy. Young men, most of whom had served in the military during the war, were running rampant around the county doing what they pleased with little fear of interference from the law.

Flo was no exception. Some of the Flo men, feeling their manhood and freedom, ran around together, barefooted and naked above the waist, with a beer in one hand, if not indeed both, and a little change in their pockets from the twenty dollars they received every week for fifty-two weeks. This income was provided to veterans of World War II who could not find a job during the readjustment period after the war. Although very meager by today's standards, this income was more than the men had received before the war, even when they had a job. Many of them were content with this handout from the government and were in no hurry to find a job while the income continued.

The idleness led to difficulties, of course. Fists, clubs, knives, and even guns were used to settle disputes between these free-wheeling men and others in the community. Sometimes the fights were between the men themselves, if no outside citizen was convenient for them to attack. Further, the physical conflicts were not limited to the Flo area. The Flo men delighted in doing things like breaking up parties or dances in other areas of the county. Men in other areas of the county were causing the same kinds of problems in their own areas.

Finally, the citizens of Leon County had enough of this frontier-days mentality and talked Ben Lee into running for sheriff. The situation had, by this time, gotten so bad that they also asked for help from the state in controlling the rampaging men. A State Patrol office was established in Buffalo, from which at least two highway patrolmen operated. Ben Lee worked with the state patrolmen when he needed help in controlling his Leon County constituents. One of the officers was an older man, not long from retirement, who was known to be one tough hombre. He beat one of the Flo toughs senseless when the Flo resident kicked him in the head from the back seat of the patrol car.

About noon on July 9, 1949, one of the witnesses to the coming event was sitting in the barber shop in Centerville, down the street a few steps from the Sullivan drugstore, which was located across the street corner from the courthouse square. One of the Leon County sheriff's deputies, Leonard Barnet, who was also the jailer, had just completed cutting Ben Lee's hair (in those days Leon County could not pay the sheriff's deputies a living wage so they also had outside jobs). When Ben left the barber shop to go about his business in Centerville, this witness took his place in the barber chair.

Ben got into his car and pulled away from the curb, headed south on Highway 75, when a loud yell was heard by several witnesses. The general consensus is that it was something like, "Come back here you son-of-a-bitch and buy me a new shirt." The voice was that of Tom Bill Featherston, not a Flo resident, but a tough young man of a similar attitude, nature and temperament to that of some of the Flo boys. There is no doubt at all that this young man was intoxicated. Ben either did not hear Tom Bill or he ignored him and drove on, reportedly to a small town south of Centerville called Leona. Thirty minutes later he came back into Centerville, heading north on Highway 75, when he again passed the point on the street where Tom Bill and his friends were gathered on the sidewalk. Again a yell was heard, and again Tom Bill cursed Ben and demanded that he buy him a shirt.

Ben immediately pulled over to the curb, got out of his car, went up to Tom Bill and advised him that he was taking him to jail one way or another. He took Tom Bill by the arm to lead him away, but Tom Bill was in no mood to be led. He was on the sidewalk with a group of his friends and sympathizers and he was ready to fight Ben Lee (they had previously had trouble as you will see shortly). Many other people were also on the street on this Saturday afternoon and watched the incident unfold. Ben and Tom Bill started scuffling and someone immediately walked the few steps to the barber shop and advised the deputy, Leonard, that Ben and Tom Bill were having trouble. The witness in the barber chair told Leonard to go ahead and leave the barber shop, but Leonard asked him to go with him. They stepped out of the barber shop and saw Ben and Tom Bill in a scuffle.

In the meantime, a crowd had gathered around Ben and Tom Bill, quite a few of which were Tom Bill's friends. One of these friends, a fellow that farmed Tom

Bill's family farm, was very upset and was saying challenging things to Ben. Leonard walked up to him and said, "I think you and I ought to stay out of this." This calmed the fellow down somewhat and he moved back from the fight, but he was still excited and did not remain entirely silent.

An older fellow in the crowd named Cliff Barnes came to Ben's aid when it appeared that Ben could not handle Tom Bill alone. Ben was at least fifty years old and was not in great physical condition. Tom Bill was much younger, weighed about two hundred pounds, and was of stocky build, perhaps five feet and ten inches in height and was obviously very strong and no stranger to a fight. Ben was on one side of Tom Bill and Cliff was on the other trying to hold him during the scuffle. They moved Tom Bill forward on the sidewalk a few steps toward the courthouse square and the jail. When they came to some concrete steps on the sidewalk that they had to climb, Tom Bill put his feet against the steps and flatly refused to go any further. During this time the excited friend of Tom Bill was telling Cliff Barnes the stay out of it because he was no lawman and had no business helping Ben.

"Where are your handcuffs?" Cliff asked Ben.

"In my car. Go get them." Why Ben didn't have his handcuffs with him no one knows, but remember this was Leon County in 1949 and he was not a professional lawman trained in modern methods for controlling a young, strong, unruly prisoner. Cliff left Ben to get the handcuffs and Leonard left Ben to call for help from the state patrolmen in Buffalo. A disaster in the making, one might say.

The scuffle between Ben and Tom Bill now became a fullfledged fight. Tom Bill told Ben that he was going to have to pay him for a shirt that Ben had apparently torn off him a week earlier during another altercation he and the state patrol officers had with Tom Bill.

Since Ben couldn't move Tom Bill, he pulled a slapjack (a type of flexible blackjack) from his pocket and rapped him on the head with it. It slowed Tom Bill down for a second or two, after which he came back fighting. Several witnesses state that the slapjack only helped sober him up. Ben hit him with the slapjack another time or two, but Tom Bill came back fighting after each blow (Ben had made the remark to someone in the past that a man his size could easily kill someone with a blackjack if he wasn't careful so perhaps he was not hitting Tom Bill as hard as he could or should).

By now Ben was disheveled, his shirt tail hanging out and his pants had slipped down so low on his hips that several witnesses thought they might drop all the way down to his shoes. During the scuffle he had lost his hat, a large white Stetson, and when it fell to the ground in front of the witness that had been in the barber shop, he said, "Pick up my hat." As the witness reached for the hat Tom Bill said, "Yes, pick up his goddamned hat!" He picked it up and laid it on the hood of a jeep that was parked near where he was standing.

About this time several witnesses were wondering whether or not they should come to the aid of Ben. They knew that if they did they would perhaps make an enemy of Tom Bill for life and they didn't relish that thought. Ben never asked for help from anyone.

During the fight, Tom Bill apparently hit Ben a hard blow causing him to wince and gasp for breath momentarily. During all this time it was noted by several witnesses that Ben kept his side on which his gun was located away from Tom Bill as best he could. Eventually Tom Bill grabbed the large end of the slapjack and, since Ben did not have it anchored around his wrist with a strap and held the small end, Tom Bill wrenched it away from him.

There are three different versions of what happened in the next few seconds. One version is as follows: Tom Bill swung the slapjack at Ben's head with great force. Ben threw up his left arm and more or less blocked the blow. If it had hit his head squarely it might have killed him. Ben hit Tom Bill in the face with his right fist as hard as he could. It knocked Tom Bill back a step or so, but he came back immediately with the slapjack. Ben drew his new .38-caliber revolver in an instant and fired at Tom Bill's head. Tom Bill ducked at just the right time and came at Ben again with the slapjack, but not in a direct approach. He turned sideways to Ben and came toward him in a semi-circular movement with his side exposed. Ben merely turned his wrist and fired again. The bullet hit Tom Bill in the ribs, about halfway between his belt and his shoulder, more toward his back than toward his front, dropping him immediately. He landed face down and never made a sound or another movement thereafter.

Another version is that when Tom Bill pulled the slapjack away from Ben, his momentum caused him to fall off the sidewalk (which was a foot or so above the ground) where he landed face down in the dirt. Ben pulled his gun and fired it accidentally, missing Tom Bill by a wide margin, but then shot him in the side of his back as he lay on his face in the dirt.

The third version is very much like the second in that Ben was on the sidewalk and Tom Bill was standing

222

on the ground several steps from him, after stumbling off the sidewalk. He was preparing to run at Ben with the slapjack drawn back to hit him when the first shot was fired. When he heard the first shot and saw the gun, he turned to the side (very few witnesses believe he was trying to run) before the second bullet hit him. In this version, when he was shot down he may have tried to hand the slapjack to a bystander with words like, "Give this to Mr. Ben."

The first bullet passed to the right of the witness that was from the barber shop, and the second would have come very close to him had not Tom Bill's body stopped it. He admits it scared him. The first bullet, whether fired accidentally or not, missed Tom Bill, passed through the door of the jeep on which Ben's hat had been laid, then out the back striking Wendel Bell in the upper arm, passing completely through his arm between the bones. He was at the back of the jeep and had his elbow on the end gate when the firing took place. The bullet then went across Highway 75 and hit a black man in the leg (Ben later paid the two wounded men's doctor bills and bought the black man a bag of groceries).

About this time the state patrolmen came roaring up to the fray, too late to help make the arrest and prevent the killing. Wendel Bell, who had felt nothing when the bullet went through his arm, went immediately to Dr. Powell's office (the Centerville doctor) when he discovered blood dripping from his fingers. The doctor started to look at his wound, but Wendel advised him to go look at Tom Bill first. He immediately went to the scene, examined Tom Bill for a moment, and told the crowd to load him into an ambulance and head for the Palestine hospital, some fifty miles away. They left a couple of minutes later, siren blaring. By the time the ambulance got to Buffalo, fifteen miles away, the ambulance driver decided that Tom Bill was dead, so they stopped at Dr. L. P. Tenney's office where he verified the death of Tom Bill.

Doctor Powell went back to his office and put something (believed to have been a sulfa drug of some sort) on the entrance and exit wounds of Wendel's arm without cleaning out the wound. Four hours later James O. Hill, another witness to the killing, had to take him to Doctor Heath in Madisonville. Wendel was in great pain and didn't want to go back to Doctor Powell. When they arrived, Doctor Heath ran a swabbing stick of some sort clear through Wendel's arm to clean out the wound. It was a very painful time for Wendel.

Back in Centerville, a group of Ben's supporters, friends, acquaintances and sympathizers were with him at the sheriff's office. Tom Bill's friends, including his emotional friend who was now near hysteria, apparently went to Tom Bill's home a couple of blocks from the courthouse square. When Ben heard the emotional friend of Tom Bill could possibly cause more trouble, he asked the state patrol officers to go get him. It was not necessary, for they got the word very soon that he had been quieted by his own people.

One of the bystanders at the shooting drove out to Bill Lee's (Ben's brother) house in Flo to tell him about what had happened. When he was told, Bill said, "I was afraid something like this might happen because I knew that he was like the rest of the Lees, and that when he took on the job he would do it to the best of his ability." Bill decided he would go to Centerville with the bystander. When he came out to his truck he asked the bystander if he had a pistol with him. He replied that he had a little .25-caliber automatic and about three old shells for it, but that it might not be very reliable. Bill decided that he didn't want it. He told him that he had tried to sneak his shotgun out of the house, but his wife caught him and she made him leave it at home. They headed for Centerville with no firepower in the vehicle.

When they got to Centerville everything was quiet and the streets were essentially deserted. They drove to Ben's house a few miles from Centerville and found it full of people with others standing outside talking in the yard. Ben's other brother, Bud Lee, was also there. He was sitting on a flatbed truck in the yard, surrounded by a crowd that liked to hear him talk. He was a great storyteller. Some concerned friend asked him if he thought Tom Bill's people or friends might try to come out to Ben's place and do him harm. "Well, I don't think so," he drawled, "but if that's what they want, then let them come."

No further conflicts concerning the death of Tom Bill occurred. Apparently the whole thing was started months earlier, when Tom Bill's brother, a one-armed man, did something at Centerville that resulted in Ben trying to arrest him. He ran and Ben followed him home, went inside and arrested him. During the chase Ben was said to have pulled his gun and tried to fire a warning shot, but the gun did not fire. He immediately ordered a new revolver, which he used later in the altercation with Tom Bill.

Later, shortly before the incident that resulted in his death, Tom Bill had an altercation with Ben and the two state patrolmen concerning a conflict he and his friends had with some carnival workers that were in town. Tom Bill was riding the Ferris wheel, again apparently intoxicated, and did something, perhaps rocking the seat he was in, which scared some Negro kids that were also on the Ferris wheel. The carnival worker stopped the ride and demanded that Tom Bill leave. He got off the ride, but demanded his money back. The carnival worker refused and a loud argument ensued. Someone from the carnival called Ben. It is also said that the carnival worker screamed the words "Hey, Rube!" and within a moment several other carnival workers swarmed around him with weapons of all kinds, ready to fight. When Ben and the state patrolmen tried to arrest him, Tom Bill managed to fight them off as they moved along the street for a couple of blocks.

One of the state patrolmen kept urging Ben to use his slapjack on Tom Bill to knock him senseless, but Ben would not do so, and apparently the state patrolmen hesitated to disable Tom Bill without Ben's consent. One of them even pulled his gun and was going to shoot Tom Bill, but Ben talked him out of it. Finally, Tom Bill got away from them and ran to his home a short distance away. Ben went back to the courthouse to obtain a search warrant for entering Tom Bill's house to arrest him. In the meantime, a precinct constable named Lucian Watson, who perhaps had been called by Tom Bill, took him to a Justice of the Peace or some other official to take care of the charges, which resulted in Tom Bill spending at least an hour or so in jail. Some believe Tom Bill went to the constable to avoid being arrested by Ben.

Whatever the truth is, it was obvious that Tom Bill Featherston hated Ben Lee, and that his actions, obviously influenced by his drinking, eventually led to his death.

Everyone in Leon County would agree that Tom Bill Featherston lived hard and died young.

51

A DAMNYANKEE COMES TO LEON COUNTY

My brother-in-law, Pete Gray, is a Yankee. I don't call him a Yankee using the usual Flo, Texas criteria for the word, which means anyone born north of Dallas. This guy is from Indiana, so that makes him the worst kind of Yankee, a DamnYankee (notice that it is a single word).

Before my father died in 1954 all three of his male children had grown up and moved away from Flo. I won't go into all the reasons why, but I can assure you they were numerous. Perhaps the main one was to get away from the type of life we had lived up until we were teen-agers, and were afraid we might have to continue to live for the rest of our lives.

After my father's death none of the three brothers would agree to come back to Flo and live on the old homestead, even though all the land that my father and mother owned was available for use, free of charge, to the one who would return. A few years passed without the old homestead being occupied by anyone.

In the meantime our sister, Edith, met this small Yankee and married him. They moved to his home in Indiana to farm. Things didn't go so well there for various reasons, primarily because Pete liked to work every day farming until around midnight, then sleep late the following morning. His father didn't keep those kinds of hours and was pecking on Pete's door about daybreak every morning, demanding that Pete get up and get with it. I guess he felt this privilege was his since he owned the farm that Pete was farming.

To make a long story short, Pete and Edith sold out in Indiana and moved to Flo to the old homestead, Pete wanting to "blend" into the Flo community (an impossibility for such a Yankee--he's still trying to blend in after more than thirty years).

One of Pete's methods of trying to blend in was to emulate a well respected, knowledgeable, no-nonsense rancher that lives in Flo named Evan Moore. Evan is only about four years older than Pete. Evan, with the stamina of a horse and the patience of Job, decided he should help his new neighbor, Pete Gray, get off to the right start in Flo.

Back in 1957, Evan owned a big ranch down on Buffalo Creek and had lots of cattle. Being a macho type guy, he handled his cows with a horse, a whip and a dog (not the way to do it, he now agrees). He wore a big cowboy hat and boots with spurs and looked like the cowboy that he actually was.

Pete Gray, the DamnYankee, wanted to look and operate just like Evan. He went to town and bought himself a ten-gallon cowboy hat. Edith said it was more like fifteen gallons since it came down to Pete's ears on the sides and down to his eyes in the front. On his way home, wearing the hat and boots, he sprained an ankle and couldn't get his boot off, so he wore them day and night for a week until his swollen ankle went back to normal size.

The day after he bought the hat and boots he went to Evan and asked him to help locate and buy a saddle horse, so that he wouldn't look out of place in Flo. Evan, in his usual efficient manner, found a horse that he thought Pete might learn to handle. When they

229

got ready to load the horse in the truck, however, it balked and they could not get it into the truck either by leading it, pushing it or whipping it on the rump. Pete decided that loading it was a physical impossibility and was ready to give up, but Evan, being an old hand, decided that he would ride the horse into the truck. He mounted the horse and tried at least a dozen times to get it into the truck. No luck. He then rode the horse out about a hundred yards, turned it around to face the rear of the truck and spurred it into a dead run. He raked it with the spurs, whipped it with his hat, and yelled his head off as he approached the truck. At the last instant the horse made a mighty leap and landed in the truck, which stopped him so quickly that Evan, had he not been a veteran horseman, would have continued over the cab of the truck.

Pete ran over and put up the tailgate of the truck and congratulated Evan on how well he could handle horses. "Nothing to it," said Evan in his usual nonchalant voice.

A few days later, Pete was riding in the woods checking the fences around one of our places when he rode up on Willie Lynch, standing on her property across the fence from our place. She had two dogs with her and was fingering a .30-caliber Winchester in a manner that Pete can describe only as "menacingly."

Willie Lynch was a widow (called "widow-woman" in Leon County), a self-made woman, independent as a Cheshire cat and was not afraid of anything in the entire world, especially the men that owned property around hers in Flo. Our father had difficulty with her for years. Her cows and hogs would sometimes get through the fence onto our place and sometimes ours would get onto her property. It was always a very delicate situation to set things right with her one way or another. She was known to shoot her rifle over your head at times, just to make sure she had your attention.

Pete knew about Willie Lynch, of course. He had heard of her from our father, from Evan and others, and from my brothers and me.

When Pete saw Willie, he proceeded to tie his horse's reins to an overhanging limb of a tree just as Evan had taught him to do, got off his horse, walked over to the fence and tried to talk to Willie. Willie could understand very little of what he was saying for she had never heard a Yankee voice in her life. I'll leave it to your imagination as to how this conversation went between this pint-sized Yankee and this Amazon of the woods named Willie Lynch.

Finally the conversation ended, or more likely stalled, and Pete turned and with great dignity walked over to his horse, put his boot in the stirrup and with what he hoped was a flourish tried to lift himself into the saddle. The stirrup broke and he ended up sitting on the ground with the stirrup in his lap.

Pete didn't look at Willie. He got up slowly, moved calmly around the horse to the other side, put his foot in the other stirrup and tried to mount the saddle a second time. The girth broke and he ended up flat on his back with the saddle on top of him. He heard choking and gasping from across the fence where Willie was trying her best to control her laughter. He still didn't look at her.

Pete untied the horse and led it away from Willie through the brush toward home. He never rode the horse again, nor did he bother to go back for the worn-out saddle.

The first year Pete lived in Flo he raised a corn crop in one of our fields. It was a good corn crop, better than most corn crops grown in Flo. Those midwesterners do know how to raise corn.

When the corn got to the roasting ear stage, Pete noticed that the raccoons were knocking it down and eating it. He could tell this from all the raccoon tracks in his cornfield. He went to his friend, Evan, to seek his advice. Evan came over and walked through the cornfield with him and told Pete that some hogs were knocking the corn down and eating some of it, and that the raccoons were coming in later and finishing it off. Pete didn't quite believe it.

Evan had a pasture leased for his cows that joined the field Pete had his corn planted on. One day he was riding his pasture and saw a wild sow with three shoats go through Pete's fence into the field. He saw that they were very fat, something rarely seen in wild hogs, and immediately knew that these hogs were the ones that had been eating Pete's corn. He told Pete about the hogs. By this time, Pete had finally become convinced that Evan had been right about the hogs eating his corn.

Pete's solution was to "gather" his corn while it was still pretty green to prevent further loss to the hogs. He rented three barns in the area and spread his corn out in the barns so that it wouldn't go bad from overheating in a fermenting process. The sow and shoats kept coming onto Pete's place, but he didn't care so much now since he had his corn in the barns.

Later in the fall, Pete and Evan noticed that there was an excellent acorn crop on all the oak trees that grow wild in Leon County. Hogs have traditionally fattened on acorns for a hundred and fifty years. Pete and another local rancher, Frank Lee, went a hundred miles south of Flo and bought two truck loads of hogs, one for Frank and one for Pete. Pete turned his hogs loose, after a few days, on the farm where he had raised the corn. He expected them to get fat over the winter by eating the acorns.

Although the wild sow that had come onto Pete's place to eat his corn was wild as a deer, she nevertheless had been marked; that is, had certain cuts in her ears to identify who she belonged to. This had been done several years before when she was a pig or a shoat. She had been running wild ever since. Evan knew how to do these things, so he found out that the sow really belonged to a Negro woman that lived in Pleasant Springs, a Negro settlement somewhere back in the woods, fairly near Pete's place. Her husband had died and another Negro man, named George Hopkins, now spoke for her at times. Evan went to him and asked him to tell the Negro lady that he and Pete would catch and return her sow to her if she would give the three shoats to Pete for their effort. A few days later he got the word that she had agreed to his offer.

In the meantime, the wild sow and her three shoats had joined up with the other hogs Pete had brought onto his place; however, they were still wild as the wind and could not be caught or penned with the other hogs.

That winter Evan and Pete got word from a Mrs. Dodds, who lived in the brush near Pete's place, that she had located the wild sow and the three shoats in the woods on Pete's farm. The next morning Evan and Pete were at her place at sunrise. Evan was on his horse, wearing leather chaps, a leather coat, a big cowboy hat and spurs on the heels of his cowboy boots. He had two hog dogs with him. You couldn't say he didn't come prepared. Pete looked like his gentlemanly self, Yankee-like, not like a Leon County redneck ready to chase a wild hog through the brush at sunrise.

Evan's plan was simple. The dogs would bay the hogs and keep them bunched. Most of the hogs were Pete's tame hogs, but the wild sow and shoats were with them and wouldn't leave the herd. Evan, ever sure of himself, took a bag of corn with him, tied to his saddle. He planned to rope the wild sow.

The dogs bayed the hogs and kept them bunched. Pete walked while Evan rode his bay mare on the way to the hogs. Evan saw a strange contraption in Pete's hand, and being a polite southerner and all, asked him something like, "What in the hell is that damned contraption you're carrying, for God's sake!"

"It's a hog catcher," replied Pete as if what he was doing made some sort of sense. Pete showed Evan the hog catcher. It was a four-foot long metal pipe with a steel cable running through it. When you pushed the cable into the pipe it formed a loop at the other end, which you slipped over a hog's snout to subdue and control him. Going wild hog hunting with it seemed to Evan about like going bear hunting with a slingshot. He didn't say anything, however, because he was so amazed that he simply couldn't talk.

They arrived at the hogs and Evan immediately went into his hog cajoling act using the corn. He spread a little corn near the hogs and they would mill about watching the dogs, which were continuously circling them and barking constantly. Finally the hogs relaxed a bit and began to eat the corn; all but the wild sow. She was eyeing the dogs and would have run for it on her

234

own, but was afraid to leave the herd because the dogs would have been on her instantly.

Evan dropped more corn. The hogs relaxed further and even the wild sow picked up a little corn and ate it. He was edging her out of the brush to where he could drop his lariat over her. Suddenly, out of the corner of his eye he saw Mrs. Dodds and her six year old granddaughter walk up.

Oh, it was a grand morning! Just like in the frontier days. There was a smell of woodsmoke in the frosty air. The rumble of a freight train passing through Buffalo, ten miles away, could be heard clearly. The dog's barking was echoing across the valleys through the woods. A cool fog was lying in the low places. The air was crisp and fresh. It was one of those unique days when you feel like shouting, just to hear your voice echo across the wilderness.

Mrs. Dodds must have felt that way too, for she suddenly let out a yell that could raise the dead. She did it not to scare the hogs, but through sheer exuberance. Some folks in Flo always thought that she might be part Indian and would have been certain of it had they been there that morning.

The hogs froze in place, their ears standing straight up. The dogs, with great difficulty, kept the hogs from bolting. Mrs. Dodds' voice kept coming back as echoes from far distant creeks, hills and valleys for what seemed to be at least five minutes.

Evan said nothing, but just dropped more corn. Soon he had the hogs settled down again and had enticed the wild sow out into the open. Just as he was ready to drop his loop over the sow, Mrs. Dodds let out another of her ear-splitting screams.

That did it. Hogs went in every direction, scattering like quail. The wild sow tore through the brush toward a place called Devil's Den, a sink hole in the creek about a half mile away. Devil's Den covers about an acre or two of marsh, quicksand, briars, trees, potholes, myrtle bushes and grass. The dogs were after her but she was outrunning them. If she could make it to Devil's Den she was home free. Ten men couldn't have gotten her out of it in a week.

Evan, feeling good and his horse feeling good, took up the chase. His horse was running full speed through the brush, dodging through it where it could and busting holes in it where it couldn't find an opening. When they had to bust through the brush, Evan would pull his hat down over his face and hang on. Pete, Mrs. Dodds, and her granddaughter were left far behind.

Just before the sow got to Devil's Den she had to pass through a small glade about thirty steps across that was free of bushes. Evan knew that if she made it across the glade she was free and clear. He removed his lariat from the horn of his saddle, shook out a small loop about three feet across and started swinging it over his head. When he broke out into the glade the wild sow was already halfway across it. He took one mighty swing of the loop and threw it at her as hard as he could. It was his last desperate shot at capturing her. Just as the lariat played out and the loop began to close, he saw the loop drop over her head, more like an accident than technical skill. When the horse saw the lariat play all the way out it slammed on its brakes. The sow ran right through the loop except for one hind foot which the lariat tightened up on. The hog now began to fight the rope and the dogs, while traveling in a circle around the horse, fighting like a tiger, slinging her head savagely at the dogs. The dogs couldn't get a grip on the sow's ears in order to hold her. Evan knew that all the sow had to do was get a bit of slack in the lariat and she would kick free of the loop, so he kept his horse backing up and turning to keep the rope tight.

Suddenly, out of the brush and myrtle bushes came Pete Gray on the dead run, hog catcher in hand, loop ready to capture this wild hog. In desperation, knowing that he would lose the hog any second, Evan screamed, "Catch her, Pete!"

Pete didn't hesitate. He dived in on the fighting sow, something even a redneck born and raised in Flo would be afraid to do, and somehow in the hubdub of barking dogs and head slinging, squealing sow, he managed to get his wire loop over the sow's snout. Evan was completely surprised. He guessed that Pete's chances were about one in a hundred, if not one in a thousand.

Pete reared back on the hog catcher and hung on like a bulldog. The sow, caught at both ends, flopped to the ground on her side. Evan got off his horse in a flash with a pigging string in his teeth and tied the sow's three loose feet together. He than added the fourth foot and had the sow at their mercy. Evan dragged the sow through the woods with his horse to a place to where they could drive the truck. Then they got the pickup truck, loaded the sow, and took her to Pleasant Springs and delivered her to the Negro lady that owned her. She took the sow to Crockett the next day and got one hundred dollars for her. Pete kept the three shoats until the following spring and sold them for seventy-five dollars each, which paid for the corn they had eaten out of his cornfield.

This little episode changed Evan's mind forever about what one small Yankee with a hog catcher could do to a three hundred pound wild sow in the brush. He swears Pete has always looked about a foot taller ever since that time. He felt so strongly about it that he went to town the very next day and ordered a hog catcher of his very own.

52

DAYLIGHT SAVING TIME

Some years ago, when the government decided that it should invent something called "daylight saving time," it had no idea of the chaos it was would create in Flo, Texas. I'm going to tell you about what this masterful decision made in the name of efficiency did to just one of the families that live there.

This family consists of a rancher and his wife, who I shall call John and Emily Banks to avoid their embarrassment and possibly save my own life in the process.

John and Emily had been hearing about daylight saving time on their radio and reading about it in the Buffalo Press for at least a month before the great day came to switch from central standard time to daylight saving time. They didn't understand what all the fuss was about, but being good honest citizens of Flo they prepared to do as the government dictated. They even got up at 2:00 a.m. to set their alarm clock and watches ahead one hour, just as Uncle Sam asked them to do. While they were doing this they were chanting, "spring forward, fall back" religiously.

The next morning John got up at his regular time by the alarm clock, got into his pickup truck and drove to his pasture, where he normally and faithfully fed his cows at 7:00 a.m. His cows weren't there waiting for him because, you see, the cows thought it was 6:00 a.m. and thought that John was not due to arrive for another hour. John couldn't understand this at all and kept looking at his watch and worrying about his missing cows.

Finally, the cows arrived at 8:00 a.m., by John's watch, and he gave them holy hell for being late. He had about fifty cows and he preached them a sermon then and there about the sin of showing up late. After all, he had more important things to do than waste an hour waiting for tardy cows. He actually told them that they would be in deep trouble if it happened again. He was still grumbling as he got into his truck and left the pasture.

The following morning John arrived at his pasture at 7:00 a.m. ready to feed his cows. To his great surprise not a cow was in sight. He sat on the fender of his truck for an hour trying to figure out what was going on. He had some terrible things to say about the government, but most of all he said terrible things about his cows such as, "They couldn't pour water out of a boot with directions on the heel saying 'turn up.'"

When the cows arrived at 8:00 a.m. John was ready. While they were all watching him, waiting for their feed, he went to his truck and removed his and Emily's alarm clock. He climbed into the bed of his truck and preached his cows another sermon. He held up the alarm clock so they could all see it and scolded them unmercifully, shouting things like, "Look at the damn clock, you lazy fools! Can't you even tell the time of day?" Needless to say he left the pasture the second morning very angry indeed.

When John got home he found his wife on the telephone. She had a big time official from the Federal Agriculture Department on the telephone and she was relentlessly chewing him out. John listened for a moment and heard her say something like, "You damn government bureaucrats have screwed up the entire Flo community with your stupid daylight saving time. My morning glories are so confused they're blooming an hour later than they used to. Not only that, you've totally confused all our livestock." She slammed the telephone down so hard it bounced several inches into the air and promptly fell off the table onto the floor.

During that summer John's cows ever so slowly learned how to estimate the time of day and began to arrive for feeding earlier and earlier until they all came every morning at 7:00 a.m., by John's watch.

Emily's morning glories must have been far more stupid than John's cows because they never did learn to bloom at 7:00 a.m. by the alarm clock, but always bloomed an hour later, at 8:00 a.m.

Everything finally settled down at last and John and Emily became accustomed to daylight saving time.

The government, ever the meddler, was not content with this arrangement and decided that John and Emily were getting along entirely too well, so it dropped another bombshell on them that fall. It had them switch back to central standard time. John and Emily haven't been entirely sane, if indeed they ever were, since that time.

53

THE DRUMSTICK

It must have been around 1975. Several families in Flo raised turkeys for the commercial market. They had all started out years before, around 1965, raising chickens for market, but when the market prices went bad, most chicken raisers dropped out and only the more robust and adventuresome ones switched to turkeys.

Raising turkeys is hard work. In most cases the wife of the family ends up doing ninety-percent of the work, perhaps aided at times by one or more Mexicans, in the United States illegally, who the Flo folks refer to unblushingly as "wet backs." The man of the house usually makes himself look busy, whether he actually is or not, by chasing around over the countryside in his pickup truck playing his macho role. He will, at least, lend a hand to the wife when something goes wrong in the turkey houses, such as when the watering, heating or automatic feeding system breaks down. He will try his best, however, to avoid having to do anything that requires him to touch a turkey.

Raising turkeys is quite different from raising other livestock, such as cattle, where you only look over the herd and feed them every couple of days. In raising turkeys, especially when the turkeys are small, you are under the gun twenty-four hours a day, seven days a week for the several months it takes to raise them from half-pound poults to fifteen or twenty pound grown turkeys ready for Thanksgiving dinner.

Many of the Flo women dreaded stepping out of their houses in the middle of a cold, windy night on their way to check the turkey houses because they were afraid they would hear 20,000 or so turkeys sneezing their heads off, which meant they had caught cold or some disease, which in turn meant that both the turkeys and the turkey owner were looking disaster in the face. This is only one example of the many crises the Flo women faced as turkey raisers.

One night in Flo, Opal Moore, a much better than average turkey raiser, got up in the middle of the night to make the rounds of her turkey houses to verify that her turkeys were doing okay and do some of the menial chores that are always waiting to be done in a turkey house. Because the visits to her turkey houses sometimes took as long as two hours, she usually had a bite to eat before she left her house. On this particular night she picked up a drumstick of fried chicken from her refrigerator, and since she could easily carry it in her hand and eat it as she walked along, she innocently stepped out her door and headed for the nearest turkey house.

She was met immediately by their three dogs. One was a little thing that a man named Joe Flynn had given her husband, Evan. It was an excellent squirrel dog, out of a great line of squirrel dogs that existed in Flo for a hundred years or so. The other two were large stock dogs that Evan used to handle his cattle and hogs.

All three dogs were jumping up and down with excitement at seeing Opal and were running around her in their pleasure. One of the big dogs got too close to her and tripped her. As she was falling, she inadvertently flipped the drumstick about ten feet into

243

the air. She hit the ground so hard that she lost her senses for a moment or so.

When Opal recovered enough to realize what was going on, she discovered that the two big dogs were on top of her fighting to kill each other. She would like to believe that each dog thought the other had tripped her and was fighting to protect her. Her common sense told her, however, that each dog thought the other had gobbled up the drumstick and were fighting each other over it in a jealous rage.

In the midst of this hullabaloo she looked over and saw the little squirrel dog chewing on the drumstick while watching the big dogs fighting to the death over it.

She finally got back on her feet, calmed the dogs and went on to the chicken houses where she found that the dog fight had caused some fifty of her prize turkeys to die from suffocation. They had piled up in a corner on top of each other, as turkeys are prone to do when they become frightened by such things as a dog fight.

54

NO LONGER A QUAIL HUNTER

When I was too young to carry a shotgun around with me, I envied my father and his brother-in-law, Arnett Allbright, when they would go quail hunting together two or three times each week during the fall and winter months. This was between the years 1930 and about 1938.

They would hunt on our farm in Flo and other nearby farms. This was back in the days when every family actually did some farming on a plot of ground ranging from garden size to a hundred acres or so. There were coveys of quail, located about a quarter-mile apart, all over the Flo area. The reason the quail propagated so well was because they had an abundance of food to eat, namely, the farmers' crops.

I couldn't wait to grow old enough and large enough to go quail hunting with my father. He wouldn't listen to my contention that I was ready until one day I killed a dove, on the wing, with my single shot .22-caliber rifle, loaded with "rat shot." Rat shot were .22-caliber shells loaded with tiny shot that was used to kill rats in and around a house or barn. The tiny pellets wouldn't penetrate a wall or the roof, therefore they could be used both inside and outside a building to kill rats and mice.

We had a bird dog, called "Lady," that was the finest quail dog I have ever known. If I were to tell you some of the tricks she would pull to outwit a covey of quail, or a single quail, you would accuse me of lying through my teeth. One thing she learned to do, for example, when she was about three years old, was to leave the trail of a covey of quail that were running (that is, wouldn't hold still but continued to run after being pointed by the dog) and circle them at a distance of at least a hundred yards from the birds. When she got to the point toward which they were running, she would creep forward with her belly almost on the ground and meet them. When they almost ran into her they would then hold, without further running, until the hunters flushed them (usually about ten feet in front of the dog).

I hunted with this dog for several years and she provided some fine hunting for me. One time she pointed this single quail out in the middle of an open field, which was rare because quail head for the nearest thicket the moment they are alerted by a hunter or his dog. When this quail got up out in the open and headed for the woods some hundred yards away, I actually chuckled aloud for you see I was one great marksman and I had a three-shot, 12-gauge, pump shotgun in my hands loaded with No. 8 quail loads. "Goodby, friend," I remember saying to this bird as he hit his peak height and leveled off for his flight to the woods.

I casually, even nonchalantly, lined up on him and pulled the trigger. I got a puff of feathers out of him, but he kept right on winging it. "Well, you lucky dog," I said to him as I pumped another shell into the chamber, lined up on him, and fired again. He let his right leg down to its full length, but his wings didn't miss a beat as he flew on. "This is ridiculous," I said to him as I pumped the third shell into the chamber and very carefully lined up on him this time because he was now about forty yards away, a fairly long shot. When I pulled the trigger I got more feathers and he let his other leg down to match the first one and flew blissfully on into the trees, his toes reaching for the ground all the way. I had wounded him with all three shots, but since I hadn't hit one of his wings, he merrily flew away. I decided that day that I would not make quail hunting my lifetime profession.

Many years later, about 1982, I was visiting Flo during the month of November. The weather was cool and misty and a very slight drizzle was falling. It was absolutely perfect weather for walking around in the damp woods with a gun in hand. I knew where the last surviving covey of quail was located on our property, so I loaded up my shotgun (double-barreled this time) and walked around trying to flush the covey. I got lucky and got them up in the thick brush where they were hiding out. They went in every direction through the brush like little buzz bombs. I fired at two different birds but missed them both. I noticed that it seemed to take me forever to get the gun up to my shoulder, point it in the general direction of where I guessed the bird to be and pull the trigger. The reason I had to guess where the birds were, was because I couldn't actually see the birds fly. All I could see was a brown streak here and there in the brush. I distinctly remember putting the whole load from one of the shots into the trunk of a foot-thick pine tree only a few feet from me as I swung the gun muzzle past it trying to catch up to a brown flash in the brown brush. I was showered with exploding bark from the pine tree.

I kept getting up the single birds after the covey broke up, and three hours later I had fired seventeen times and didn't have a single quail to show for my effort. I realized right then, for the first time, that it's hell to grow old.

I fired one more time at quail that day, my eighteenth shot. This quail was flying from left to right behind the standard and expected wall of brush. I followed him as best I could with the shotgun and pulled the trigger. The gun fired and I watched carefully, but didn't see the quail fall. I stood there about five seconds, feeling old and bitter, when all of a sudden I saw movement about ten feet above and in front of me. When I looked up I saw the top of a pine tree falling directly toward me. The pine was about the size of a fairly large Christmas tree that one might buy for his home. It knocked me flat. When I managed to crawl from beneath it I discovered that I had put one of the loads into the trunk of the pine where the trunk was about the size of a man's wrist, cutting the pine into two pieces, the top part which had fallen on me. Believe me, I did no more hunting that day or since.

It's just as well that I don't try to hunt quail in Flo anymore. There are very few remaining. No one farms there now, it's all cattle country, and the quail wouldn't have access to farmers' crops which they need to survive. Even worse is the fact that quail are ground nesting birds and the fire ants, which now inundate Leon County, would drive them crazy, if not indeed kill them, if they tried to nest there.

55

CHANGING TIMES

By the middle of the nineteen-eighties, Leon County had become so modernized that the more progressive people in Flo and the surrounding area decided they needed a public water system. The system was to consist of the water line itself, as well as huge water tanks and associated pumping stations located every few miles along the two-lane paved roads and the one-lane dirt roads that meandered through the area.

Leon County has no system of roads that are laid out along section lines in a grid-like pattern, as is the case in many areas of the United States. One could easily believe that the present roads were laid out along paths followed by some hog, cow, drunken cowboy, sod buster, one of Santa Anna's wounded Mexican soldiers, or perhaps a primitive Kickapoo Indian way back in time.

For two hundred years before this more or less modern water system was put in, each farm house had either a "dug" well or a "bored" well in the front yard (before the well was put in water was carried from a nearby spring or creek). A dug well was about four feet in diameter and went down no more than about fifty feet into the ground to where water was found. You "drew" water from the well by hand, using a rope, bucket and overhead pulley. A bored well was different from a dug well only in that it was about eighteen inches in diameter.

Starting around 1960, after electricity came to Flo, some of the more prosperous farmers and ranchers put in deep wells, perhaps six hundred feet deep, from which massive amounts of water could be brought to the surface by electrical pumps. By the nineteen-eighties, many of the Flo citizens had been exposed to the modern life and they demanded something better than the individual wells system; that is, they wanted a public water system.

The Flo Community Water Service Company was established to put the project into existence and operation and the work was started. The members of the water board were local people that everyone in the area was acquainted with and, in many cases, was related to in some way, either by blood or through marriage.

Many residents had no plan to ever hook up to the water line that passed their homes and continuously fought the existence of the water line on their property. This resulted in the expected conflict between some fiercely independent Flo area old-time residents and what they considered a Johnny-come-lately bunch of ignorant, inexperienced, bureaucratic do-gooders out to destroy their serentiy, if not indeed their entire way of life.

Typically, but not always (this being Leon County), an easement about fifteen feet from the edge of the road right of way was obtained from the landowners by the water service company. A bulldozer would push its way through the trees and brush, knocking everything flat, to open a path. It would be followed by a ditch-digging machine which would dig a trench about three feet deep, into which the four-inch diameter plastic water line was placed.

From time to time the water service company would have trouble with a local resident for any one of a dozen or so reasons. They would not have obtained an easement from the land owner before trespassing on his land (which could have gotten the trespasser killed some fifty years earlier), the owner would refuse them an easement, or the owner would object to one thing or another that the engineering crew or the construction crew had done that dissatisfied him. Some of these conflicts got pretty serious and even resulted in the water line being deliberately cut by someone to show their displeasure with the line and those responsible for installing it.

It took a few years to install the basic system and additional water lines are even now being added to service new residents moving into the county and the Flo area.

The furor over the water line has now disappeared and more and more residents, even the older ones, have learned to live with the new water system and appreciate its advantages.

The modernization of the Flo community and surrounding areas continue. It all started at the end of World War II with the paving of a two-lane road through the Flo crossroads, followed by the installation of electric power lines, telephone lines, and water lines. I wouldn't be surprised to hear soon that cable TV lines are scheduled to be installed next. Even in Leon County, Texas these are changing times.

56

THE PET DONKEY

I was talking to a gentleman I'll call Ben Johnson who I met in Centerville, which is about ten miles from Flo, when he learned that I am a writer. Right away he wanted to tell me a true story.

"Let me tell you about an unpredictable little pet donkey that spent a few years in Flo before he finally got into trouble and was moved out of the community," he said to me. He eyed me for a while to see if I appeared to be interested. My interest must have been obvious for he continued his story.

"Once a year for several years a celebration of sorts called the "Buffalo Stampede" has been held in Buffalo. At first it lasted for about three days, but may not last that long now. People from all over the county come and bring all kinds of things, from animals of various sorts to cars, decorated bicycles, different kinds of floats and so forth, which they enter into a big parade and march about town. It's like a combination county fair and carnival. On one of the three days they have a trail ride in which dozens of men, women and children ride their horses, mules, donkeys, buggies, and wagons on a twenty mile ride. Somewhere along the route they stop at a ranch and have a meal. One of the days they also have a big country and western type dance. During the celebration, in order to raise money for worthy causes, they have an auction in which items people have donated are auctioned off, including animals.

"One of the animals auctioned off for two or three years in a row was a very small donkey, one of those little Mexican burros, that was an ideal pet. Some years, the person that outbid the others for this little pet would return it to the auction ring immediately and it would be resold two or three times, each time bringing several hundred dollars. It was a real money raiser.

"In 1986 one of the Cash brothers (not their real name), either Barry or Gene, who have some acreage in Flo where they spend weekends, was involved in the bidding for this little donkey and before he knew it he was the proud owner of the donkey and was about three hundred and fifty dollars poorer.

"He took the donkey to his place in Flo and put it into his pasture, intending to sell it at the Buffalo Stampede the following year. For some reason he failed to return it to the auction ring and it stayed on the Cash's place another year or so.

"In the meantime, the Cashs had grandchildren that were coming along and the grandchildren played with the lovable little donkey, that was only about three feet tall, on weekends when they came to Flo. The donkey was so gentle that the grandchildren, starting when they were about four years old, fed it all kinds of things, crawled all over it and under it, and rode it at times. The donkey was very patient and kind to the kids.

"One day, at the Cash's request, one of their neighbors brought his prize Hereford bull, that weighed about sixteen hundred pounds, to the Cash's place to service their cows. He backed his trailer containing the bull up to the opened gate, got out of his truck, and opened the trailer to let the bull out. The bull was a little nervous as a result of the ride in the trailer and the fact that he was in a strange place.

"Just as the bull started to leave the trailer, there came a blood-curdling cry from the pint-sized donkey. If you have never heard a donkey bray, at close range, you have no idea how horrifying it can be. It's at least as bad as hearing a wild bull elephant trumpeting next to your tent in the middle of a dark night in the bush in Africa.

"The bull had never seen a donkey in his life, much less heard one bray, and it scared him half to death. He bolted from the trailer, ran right through the cows waiting for him and continued across the pasture. It never occurred to him, that he had passed through some love-starved cows. To the neighbor's complete surprise, he saw the little donkey chasing his bull while braying at maximum volume about every twenty steps. Watching a sixteen hundred pound bull run from a two hundred pound donkey was a sight to behold. The bull came to the fence across the pasture, turned left, and ran pell-mell through the brush, alongside the fence, with the braying donkey on his tail.

"The neighbor guessed what was about to happen so he listened closely. Soon he heard the twang of barbed wire in a fence that has just been hit by a massive bull. He had hit the fence at the end of the pasture.

"A few seconds later the bull reappeared in the brush coming back toward where his owner stood. His nose was bleeding. Right behind him, braying insanely, was this devil of a donkey. The bull finally tired, stopped and turned to face the donkey, preparing to put up a fight as all good bulls worth their keep will do when they must.

"The little donkey danced in like a master swordsman might do, somehow missed the bull's head,

and jumped up and grabbed the top of the bull's neck'
with his teeth just forward of the bull's shoulders.

"The bull began to turn in a circle as fast as he
could trying to get to the donkey with his head. He was
much taller than the donkey so the donkey's hoofs were
off the ground most of the time. What you should
understand here is that a donkey fights with his teeth,
not his heels like a horse will do. When a jack grabs
something or someone with his teeth he simply won't let
go. He hangs on like a bulldog.

"About this time, the neighbor yelled back across
the pasture to his granddaughter, who had stayed with
the truck and trailer at the gate. He told her to go get
his son, who was at the neighbor's ranch house a half
mile away, and have him bring the shotgun. He also
told her that the donkey was killing his bull, which was
far from the literal truth, but he didn't have time for
explanations.

"He looked back at the behemoth vs. dwarf fight
just in time to see his bull finally get his head under the
donkey and pitch him straight up in the air. The donkey
was spreadeagled in the air above the bull's back, but he
still had his teeth clamped on the bull's neck.

"Out of the corner of his eye the neighbor saw his
truck and trailer going about ninety miles an hour down
the dirt road, raising a cloud of dust, on the way for
help. He was proud at that particular moment that his
granddaughter was not a timid soul, even though she
had put his truck and trailer in grave danger.

"Back to the fight. When the donkey hit the
ground after being thrown into the air, his teeth slipped
off the bull's neck. The bull now headed for his owner,
but had to keep turning in order to keep his head facing

the donkey. The donkey kept trying, but he couldn't get past the bull's head to get another bite with his teeth.

"About this time the son arrived with the shotgun. Seeing that at last the bull was holding his own, the neighbor said, 'Don't kill him unless he gets another hold on my bull.'

"The bull and donkey edged across the pasture, still circling each other, toward the gate where the bull had been unloaded. Finally, the neighbor and his son maneuvered them around to the point where they could let the bull out of the gate and close the gate on the donkey. They were separated at last and the neighbor and son drove the bull down the road back to their ranch.

"Being an old stockman, the neighbor tried to figure out why this little toy-sized donkey had gone beserk and attacked a bull at least eight times as large as himself. He finally decided that the donkey had not been castrated properly; he had seen some evidence of this during the fight, and that the donkey did not want any other male animal in the same pasture with him. Something about this continued to bother the neighbor, however, for he could not forget the viciousness with which the little donkey had attacked his huge bull.

"One day, during the week, when the Cashs were absent, he went to their place to feed some of their stock, including the little donkey. He found one of their cows with her tongue hanging out, so lacerated and swollen that she could not retract it into her mouth. He called a veterinarian who came and trimmed and cleaned the cow's tongue, gave her a shot, and stated that the only thing that it might be was something called 'woody tongue.' Although they didn't discuss it, they both suspected that the cow had been attacked by another animal or perhaps a man.

"Three days later the cow died because she could neither eat nor drink. The neighbor tied a rope to her and dragged her to the far corner of the wooded pasture with his tractor. When the Cashs came in that weekend he told them what had happened, and that he believed the little donkey had killed the cow and was a danger to their grandchildren, if not indeed to the Cash family adults themselves. He remembered that years earlier a big jackass had clamped his teeth on the back of the neck of a man named Frank Coldiron, a resident of Flo, and tried to pull him into the pen with him where he probably would have killed him. Frank, who was a young man and very strong, a real *hombre*, braced himself against the fence and simply refused to be dragged into the pen. A friend of Frank, a fellow livestock trader, was in the area and, when he saw that Frank was in trouble, came running over to help him. The friend's name was Charlie Henson and he was a little fellow, about five feet tall, and was extremely excitable and emotional in a crisis. He was jumping up and down near Frank, making funny sounds. Finally he asked Frank if he should get a club and hit the donkey with it. 'Hell no,' replied Frank, 'cut the bastard's throat with your pocket knife!' Charlie managed to get his knife ready and when he took a swipe at the donkey's throat the jack dodged the knife and he lost his grip on Frank's neck. Later, Frank apologized to his wife about the fact that he had not believed her, and had actually laughed at her, when she had told him that the jack had tried on several different occasions to grab her with his teeth when she was in the process of feeding him.

"The neighbor's warning went unheeded by the Cash family, for at the very time he was warning them, their grandchildren were again playing with the little docile donkey.

"The Cashs noticed, however, that once in a while the little donkey, with his teeth bared, would make a run at a calf or a cow around the place. The calf or cow would have to scramble to get away from him. One day the donkey ran a cow past Gene Cash and was biting her about the jaw. Gene broke up the attack using a club and decided then and there that the donkey had to go. When he called the neighbor and asked him what he should do, he was told that he should put a rope on the donkey, lead it to where the dead cow lay, tie it to a tree, back off about ten steps and blow the little monster to kingdom come with his deer rifle. The neighbor is no wimp; he knew exactly what should be done.

"The Cashs couldn't do it. After all, it had been their little pet for a few years and had never once attempted to harm one of their grandchildren.

"Gene Cash went to the Flo store, the social contact point for the community, and put out the word that the little donkey would be given, at no cost, to anyone that would take him. It is also reported that he put out the word that the donkey could be dangerous to other animals and kids as well.

"Right here is where the story begins to get sticky, because if the word about the donkey being dangerous doesn't get passed along to all its future owners for some reason, any reason (whether deliberately or not), then you have the makings of a real disaster. If the disaster then occurs, the question of moral and legal responsibility for the donkey's future actions arises. Big

258

lawsuits have resulted from far less complicated and serious matters.

"The donkey's ownership changed twice after it left the Cash's. It first went to a rancher that lives in the Flo area, then a short time later, to a family with two small boys that lives in Oakwood, a town about fifteen miles from Flo. As you may have surmised by now, this family did not get the word that the donkey could be dangerous. I do not know where the failure in communication occurred.

"In any event, the Oakwood family accepted the apparently harmless little donkey and their two small boys, perhaps four and six years old, along with other children in the area, began to play with it and ride it around their place every day.

"The inevitable happened. I won't go into the details here to protect the four-year old boy that was involved, other than to say that he was severely injured by the pet donkey and ended up in a Dallas hospital after the nearest hospital, in Palestine, Texas, decided they were incapable of handling his injury. The boy is quite well now, in 1993, and shows no physical or emotional evidence that he was ever harmed.

"While the boy's parents were in the hospital in Dallas with their son, his father called a friend and asked him to destroy the donkey. This donkey must lead a charmed life for the friend did not destroy the donkey, but gave him to a black man in Buffalo, another town in Leon County some fifteen miles west of Oakwood.

"That's the end of the story as far as I know it," said Ben.

"Do you know what eventually happened to the donkey?" I asked.

"No, I don't. Let's hope someone destroys him before he injures, or perhaps kills, another child."

I couldn't let the story end here of course. I talked to the injured boy's mother and she told me the name of the person in Buffalo that the donkey had been given to. I drove to Buffalo and talked to him. He had given, or perhaps sold, the donkey to another man, a cowboy type, that works at the Buffalo sale barn where a stock auction is held every week. He checked the sales records and told me that the little donkey had been sold, through the sale barn, three or four times during the year that had passed since the donkey had been given away by the friend of the family in Oakwood. As a matter of fact, he told me that the donkey had been sold at the sale barn the previous week. I asked him to provide me with the name of the present owner and his address. The present owner lives in the New Baden, Texas area some forty miles west of Buffalo.

I told the injured boy's grandmother, who lives near Flo, that the donkey was alive and well and where it was located. She, of course, passed the information on to the boy's parents. Later the boy's father drove to New Baden to verify that it was indeed the donkey that had injured his son.

At the present time (the spring of 1993) the little donkey is still in New Baden. His owner has resisted all efforts by the injured boy's parents and grandmother to have him destroyed. The owner states that the donkey is "isolated" to the extent that he cannot harm another child. You can imagine how much faith the boy's parents and his grandmother put in that declaration. They continue to try to find a way to force the donkey's owner to destroy him. They can't bear the thought of this pet donkey injuring, or perhaps killing, another child.

57

THE TELEPHONE MAN

After the people at the dinner party had waited for me to finish my dessert--I was running a little slow you understand, what with all the food and my talking too much--and we had moved back into the living room, Opal Moore told me another true story.

"I have a middle-aged cousin named Irma who lives close to the Trinity River with her ninety-four year old mother. She is a very serious and intent person and seldom engages in any sort of levity.

"One day their telephone rang and when she answered it a man's voice told her that he was a telephone lineman and asked her if she would help him locate a problem on the line. She agreed to help if she could.

"He asked her to blow into the telephone real hard. She did this and was thanked for helping. The only problem was that she needed to do it again, only harder this time. She took a deep breath and blew into the telephone about as hard as she thought she could.

"The voice again thanked her and stated that he just about had the problem solved, but that he needed one last effort from her, a mighty blast of air this time. She complied with all the air she could summon and almost blew the telephone out of her own hand.

"The voice came on the line for the last time and said, 'Thanks, lady, you just blew all the bird shit off the telephone lines for miles around!'

"My cousin hadn't cracked a smile the entire time she was telling me about this incident. She is one dead serious lady.

"She looked at me solemnly and declared in her no-nonsense voice, 'I'll tell you one damn thing; I'm never going to talk to another man claiming to be a telephone lineman as long as I live!'"

58

HELP FROM A BLACK FAMILY

There is a Negro community located eight miles or so south of Flo, called Hopewell. I remember passing through it as a boy in the back of my father's pickup truck. I remember that even then I noticed how poor the land and houses were and saw colored men following plows pulled by mules, trying to raise crops in the sandy soil. The mules were not unique to the Negro community, however, for we had mules that pulled our plows as well.

Today there is a paved farm road that goes through the Hopewell community where the old dirt road once ran. There are about a dozen houses visible from the road. A few of the houses are made of brick now, but most of them are more modest. The community still shows signs of poverty and tough living conditions.

There is a black lady named Adeline Handsborough that lives in this community and has lived there for years who, over the years, performed domestic duties for several different white ladies that live in Flo. In addition, she has helped take care of aged white ladies who were sick or disabled.

I first met Adeline about twenty-five years ago when she worked for my sister and my mother, who lived in separate houses about one-fourth mile apart. Later, after my mother became disabled, Adeline spent many hours taking care of her.

I had written a short novel in 1985 entitled THE EBONY STRIKEOUT ACE about a black man and his relationship with a white man over the period of one summer. The white man was an outfielder with the Corsicana Bandits professional baseball team and he discovered that the black man, a Trinity River fishing guide, could throw a baseball at the incredible speed of 107 miles per hour (faster than even Bobby Feller) with perfect accuracy. The setting for the story was in Oakwood, a small town in Leon County, twenty miles from Hopewell. In trying to be super realistic I had filled the story with all kinds of racist remarks made by the white men and by the Negro characters in the story. I never tried to get the story published for I didn't know how black people, young and old, rich or poor, would react to the language I had used, even though it was the language used by whites and blacks in Leon County in 1951, the time of the story.

Being in Flo for six weeks doing a bit of research for a future book, I contacted Adeline and provided her with a draft copy of THE EBONY STRIKEOUT ACE. I asked her to read it and to let others in her community read it as she desired. I specifically asked her to have her well-educated daughters read it. The daughters had gone to various colleges, with Adeline's and her husband's help, and obtained degrees and now have professional jobs such as teaching school.

Adeline agreed and kept the story for a week or so. When she returned it to me she stated that several of them had read the story, discussed it, and that their conclusions about it were written on a note attached to the front of the manuscript. I read the note, which had been written by her daughter, Doris, with some concern.

The note informed me that they had all liked the story, but that most of the racist language that I had used (albeit while quoting characters in the story) was completely uncalled-for and unnecessary. I had known this all along, but had just never admitted it to myself. They could have, but did not, accuse me of being a racist that had put my words in the mouths of my characters under the guise of being "realistic."

I feel that their reaction to my story and their lady-like response to me shows something of the character of Adeline's family. I am grateful to them for their help and have revised the story. It is now being offered to publishers for publication. If the story is ever published, I will provide Adeline with a copy of the book.

59

THE HOPEWELL NEGRO CHURCH

Part of the process of becoming reacquainted with a place and its people, after having been absent from it for more than fifty years, is to go to places where a large percentage of the local residents meet periodically. Although Flo has a community center now, where various activities take place, I decided that the best places to go were to the local churches scattered a few miles apart across the countryside in the Flo area. On five consecutive Sundays in the spring of 1992 I attended church services at the Flo Community Church, the North Creek Baptist Church, the Siloam Baptist Church, the Buffalo Baptist Church and the Hopewell Missionary Baptist Church, in that order.

Have you readers not of African descent ever attended a Negro church, way out in the country, where you had not been specifically invited by the church authorities, and attended the church alone where you were the only non-black in the congregation? I can assure you that it is quite an enlightening experience.

During one of my conversations with Adeline Handsborough, I asked her if she thought it would be appropriate for me to attend services at her church. She said that she thought that it would be all right but that she would speak to one of the deacons of the church and perhaps the pastor as well. I never got direct word from her that I should come or not come, so one Sunday morning at 11:00 a.m. I pulled into the church parking lot, ignored my misgivings, opened the door of the church and walked in. There must have been at least seventy people inside.

It happened that some church activity was just ending, perhaps Sunday School. Soon, many dark smiling faces were looking into my white face and many black hands were shaking my white hand and welcoming me to their church services. I met what appeared to be the church deacons, which were older black men dressed in business suits. I distinctly remember that I felt ridiculous in my cowboy clothes. I had brought no suits to Flo with me since I had no previous thought of attending church services anywhere, especially in a Negro church.

Soon an elderly, tall, dignified man approached me with a Bible in his hand and welcomed me to the services. He was Reverend H.U.S. Banks, who comes twice each month from Bryan, Texas, seventy miles away, to hold services in Hopewell. This is remarkable for a man that is eighty-eight years old and has been a pastor for fifty-eight years.

It must have been obvious that I didn't know much about church services and the sequence of events that take place. Soon various people in the congregation, including Adeline, began to advise me in a quiet voice from time to time about what was the appropriate thing for me to do, such as where I was to sit. They were treating me with the utmost respect.

Soon it was time to begin the morning worship service and it began with singing. Various ladies and men would lead off and others would join in. I noticed that a group of some ten ladies and a few men came out of the congregation and moved into the choir area behind the pastor and the singing continued. After a

267

few songs they returned to their seats and other ladies and men took their places. A young man named Drew Morrow comes all the way from Palestine, about forty miles away, to play the piano in the church. Although he had told me before the service started that he had no formal training in music, he could play the piano very well indeed.

The singing was followed by the offering. I thought I was prepared, but not knowing the routine I probably made about a half dozen mistakes, at least two of which I recognized myself, much too late to correct. When the small bowl came my way I noticed that the two men ahead of me put coins in the bowl, but I had several small bills in my hand and I had no time to replace them with coins, so I put the bills in the bowl. I noticed that the gentleman passing the bowl appeared to be startled at what I had done. I think this collection was supposed to be a coin collection only, for the Sunday School children or for some other worthy cause, but I had already blown it before I realized my mistake. A couple of minutes later the gentleman that had carried the bowl came by and whispered to me that there was another collection about to be made and that I need not participate further unless I cared to do so.

I ended up confused about the second collection. Some members of the congregation would come up and place their donation on a table where the deacons sat. I managed to slip the gentleman that carried the bowl a few more small bills, which he also placed on the table with money he had collected from others. The deacons then counted the donations and announced to the congregation how much money had been collected. In the meantime, the gentleman that had carried the bowl came over to me and had me verify that my name was indeed "Taylor." I wondered why at the time.

Now that the offering was completed, one of the deacons read the announcements. To my surprise, he identified me and asked me to stand and say a few words. I stood, identified myself and stated that I was from Colorado and was the grandson of Dr. W. F. Taylor who had practiced medicine between 1895 and 1925 in the area, including Hopewell, and who had been the doctor for several families that lived in Hopewell during that period. To my great relief I saw and identified an eighty-nine year old black man in the congregation, named Gus Haley, whom I had met a few days earlier. Haley remembered my grandfather and had told me that my grandfather had been his family doctor. At least I had found someone who could verify my story.

I can just imagine what about ninety-nine percent of the congregation thought of my little speech since almost all of them had been born years after my grandfather died in 1925 (later several persons told me that they had heard of my grandfather). I did at least have the presence of mind to say that I was pleased to attend their services.

All this was followed by more singing, then a reading of the Scripture, then a prayer, and more singing. I'll have to admit it; I like music and I caught myself keeping time with my feet and my hands as the singing went on and on.

The sermon was next and I thought at first that I would have trouble hearing Reverend Banks as he talked very softly. It was during this time that he talked about me and welcomed me to his service.

I assumed, incorrectly, that Reverend Banks' soft voice was due to his advanced age, but he soon changed my mind for once he got into his sermon he projected his voice very forcefully and skillfully throughout the church. I congratulated him later about his lung capacity and he seemed pleased. He delivered a good message and later I told him so.

The sermon was followed by a call to dicipleship and then adjournment. The adjournment consisted of everyone joining hands, raising them, and singing "God Be With You Till We Meet Again." It was a very moving finale to a most interesting service. The service had lasted for two hours and ten minutes.

Immediately after the service ended, one of the ladies asked me if I would stay for lunch. I told her I had to leave, but a few minutes later Adeline's daughter, Verdene, brought me a covered plate. When I got back to the house I was staying at I uncovered it, thinking perhaps it would be a piece of pie. It turned out to be a full meal, which I ate immediately. It was delicious.

All in all it turned out to be a great experience for me. I plan to go back to this church at the first opportunity.

I would recommend that at least once in your lifetime, even though you may not be of African descent, that you attend a service way out in the country in a Negro church. You'll never meet friendlier people, you'll never regret it, and you'll certainly never forget it.

60

LEON COUNTY, NO MEDICAL UTOPIA

There is not a single hospital in Leon County, Texas.

The nearest hospitals are located in the largest towns in adjacent counties, and in Corsicana, two counties away. These towns range from twenty-five to seventy-five miles from the center of Leon County. Needless to say, when you have a life-threatening medical emergency in Leon County the victim's life is in grave danger for some time just trying to get to one of the hospitals. He may even be in grave danger after he arrives, as you may surmise shortly.

Unfortunately, most residents of Leon County, being a rural population, think of these hospitals as representing the pinnacle of medical technology, knowledge, professionalism and expertise. In fact, they do not differentiate between these hospitals and the greatest specialized hospitals in the largest cities in the country. Perhaps it is just as well they have such faith in these establishments, because about ninety-nine percent of all emergency cases coming out of Leon County end up in one of these hospitals.

The problem is that, due to the Leon County resident's ignorance of emergency medical matters and procedures, inferior and substandard treatment may very well be provided to a patient without ever being detected by the family involved. If the patient is lost, then by definition he would have been lost in the largest and most specialized hospital in Dallas or New York City. To have a Leon County resident question the hospital or demand an investigation into their medical practices and procedures is almost unheard of.

Once in a great while there can be an exception, of course. I am now going to present you with an example of one of these rare occurrences.

On January 2, 1993, a sixty-two year old man in Flo began to have a heart attack at his home. Fortunately, his wife is a nurse and a certified Emergency Medical Technician (EMT), and she recognized the classic signs and symptoms immediately: chest pain, shortness of breath, nausea and vomiting, paleness, weakness, and profuse sweating. Their daughter, who is also an EMT, was present at the time and also diagnosed his problem as a heart attack.

His wife did not call for an ambulance to come to her house because she knew there was an excellent chance that the ambulance driver would become lost in the back roads in the area where she lived, and even if he didn't get lost it would be at least an hour before he arrived. Instead, she placed her husband in her daughter's car and had her drive him through the back roads to a nearby town, which was on the way to a hospital in an adjacent county. Before leaving she called the hospital and asked them to send an ambulance to meet her daughter and husband. She advised them of the nature of the problem.

She then jumped into her own car and roared off to the town where her daughter was to meet the ambulance, hoping to get there by the time the ambulance arrived.

When she arrived her husband was already in the ambulance. She immediately began having trouble with the paramedic that was in the ambulance, because he had not put her husband on oxygen nor elevated his head, the first things that should have been done. Instead, he was interviewing her husband about his past medical history and asking him mundane bureaucratic questions not directly related to the heart attack he was having. One question he asked was whether her husband was an emphysema patient. He obviously was not, and any properly trained paramedic would have known that just by observing the patient.

By this time her husband had been in the ambulance for ten minutes with no treatment whatever. At this point she demanded that her husband be put on oxygen with his head elevated, and that the ambulance leave immediately for the hospital. She considered the lack of action as gross negligence on the part of the paramedic.

Her next problem was with the ambulance driver. He drove along with the normal traffic without having his overhead emergency lights on. She, being a nurse and an EMT, knew that the Emergency Medical Service (EMS) law states that when a patient is being transferred, the lights must be on. She later checked the EMS report and it showed that they had the lights on while going to meet the patient, but did not have them on while taking the patient to the hospital.

She thought that when her husband finally arrived at the hospital that ignorance and incompetence would have been left behind and medical knowledge and technical skill would have taken over. Not so.

The emergency room doctor gave her husband something for nausea and vomiting. He then had the laboratory do a cardiac enzymes test. He came out to her and said, "Your husband isn't having a heart attack because his cardiac enzymes are normal." She was stunned to say the least for she knew that cardiac enzymes do not start to elevate until some six hours *after* damage to the myocardium (the muscular tissue of the heart). She felt that if the doctor didn't know this, he was not capable of treating her husband.

"We are transferring him, right now, to the hospital in Tyler," she said to the doctor.

"No, we have rules here. He can see a cardiologist tomorrow," the emergency room doctor said.

"I will sign a release for my husband or whatever else I have to do. You can arrange the transfer, or I will, but he's being transferred to the Tyler hospital immediately."

During all the activity at the hospital emergency room, her husband was continuing to show signs and symptoms of a heart attack. The hospital records show that forty-nine minutes passed after the emergency room doctor had talked to the doctor in Tyler before the emergency room doctor called an ambulance to transfer the patient.

After she forced the transfer to the Tyler hospital, she thought her problems with incompetence were over. Wrong! She discovered that the ambulance ran a transfer code, meaning they again drove along as if they were taking someone to a nursing home, following normal traffic with no emergency lights operating. This should have been an *emergency* transfer.

When they arrived at the Tyler hospital things were quite different. The cardiologist there stated to her that if proper treatment had been started at the first hospital, her husband would have received less heart damage. He also told her husband later that the good Lord must have been watching over him.

Her husband underwent quadruple bypass heart surgery four days later.

On her travels around the area where she first took her husband to the hospital, she noticed that there were several large signs scattered around, including one at the hospital itself proclaiming the hospital to be the mender of broken hearts and that help was just a heartbeat away. She agrees that the hospital has a good cardiologist, but believes that if the emergency room at the hospital can't recognize a heart attack when it's staring them in the face, then what chance does the patient have of living long enough to ever see the cardiologist?

After she came home following the surgery, she found a courteous letter from the first hospital, which they send to all patients that use the emergency room, asking for comments and suggestions. I'll leave it to your own judgment as to what her reply was, which she sent to the emergency room doctor, the Hospital Administrator, the President of the Hospital Board, the American Medical Association, and the Emergency Medical Service.

She is a very religious lady, a true believer. Her husband is a Baptist Minister. She is convinced that her family's prayers, as well as the prayers said at six different churches, helped spare her husband's life. Her husband needed no blood transfusion at all during the bypass surgery. Four bypasses and no blood required! She considers it a miracle. Don't try to tell this lady that God won't answer your prayers and protect you and your loved ones from arrogance, ignorance and incompetence!

Having read this story so far it should now be obvious that the general emergency patient from Leon County is at the complete mercy of the medical system, or rather the lack of a competent, professional, efficient medical system, that exists in that area. Can you even imagine the intestinal fortitude, guts if you will, it took for this lady to take on the entire system, including a *hospital*, trying to save her husband's life?

I return to Leon County almost every year, staying from perhaps a week to as long as two months. I hope that I never have a medical emergency while I am there.

61

THE WOOD THIEVES

This is a contemporary story about a fairly typical resident of Flo that simply refused to be intimidated or bulldozed into submission by a family of thieves from the Dallas area. What makes it even more remarkable is the fact that this resident is a woman living way out in the woods. Her motto might very well be "Don't Tread On Me," and she would take on the whole world if need be to protect her family, land and property.

On January 2, 1993, a sixty-eight year old man living in the Midway area near Flo had a heart attack and was taken to the Mother Francis Hospital in Tyler, Texas by way of a different Texas hospital. He had quadruple bypass surgery and remained in the hospital for two weeks.

His wife, a nurse, stayed with him at the hospital during the two-week period before bringing him home on Saturday, January 16. They were both glad to be back to what they expected to be the peace and quiet of their country home and wooded acreage.

After they arrived home she discovered that her husband had an unusually fast heartbeat and she hoped that it would drop back to normal after he settled down. Instead, his heart rate increased during the night. She spent a good part of that night and the next day, Sunday, on the telephone with her husband's doctor in Tyler and the local pharmacist in Buffalo obtaining a drug that would slow and strengthen his heart.

Later that day one of her daughters came to her house and advised her that someone was cutting wood on her land. She left her husband in her daughter's care and with her ten year old grandson went to check out the woodcutters. She came upon a man about thirty years old (who will be referred to hereafter as Wood Thief Jr.), sawing wood with a chainsaw at the edge of the woods near the road that ran across her property. A woman about his own age was loading the wood that he had cut into short lengths into the bed of their pickup truck and into a trailer hooked to the truck. Wood Thief Jr. had neither heard her drive up nor realized she was in the area. He continued his ear-splitting rape of the woods. Rest assured that this lady landowner, with a sick husband, was in no mood for playing games with these two thieves.

"What do you two think you're doing?" she asked the woman over the scream of the chainsaw.

"Cutting us a little jag of wood," was her reply.

"Who authorized it?"

"My boyfriend's father owns the land," she said, motioning in the general direction of the man with the chainsaw.

"No, it's my land."

"Oh, I think I made a mistake. Our land is over there," she said, pointing across the road.

"No. That's my neighbor's land and I happen to know that she wouldn't trade it for a gold mine. "

"Well, we own some land around here somewhere," she replied, gesturing in all directions.

"Get your boyfriend with the saw over here and do it now," she said.

The wood-loading lady went to Wood Thief Jr. and brought him over to where the landowner stood. In the meantime, her ten-year old grandson had recorded the license number of the thief's truck. The man repeated the woman's assertion that they were only "cutting a little jag of wood."

"In a full-sized pickup truck pulling a long trailer? What's your name?"

"I don't have to give you my name."

"Right! I have the license number of your truck and I'll find out what your name is by using it." At this point he relented and gave her his name, address and telephone number. She had him write this information down in the event she needed it later for legal purposes. He lived in Lancaster, Texas, not far from Dallas. She ordered him off her property, allowing them to take the wood they had already loaded in the truck and trailer. She thought that would be the end of the matter, but she was wrong. It was barely the beginning.

Shortly thereafter, the lady learned from five neighbors and acquaintances, plus members of a county road crew that were was repairing the road across her land, that several woodcutters had been seen cutting wood on her land for almost the entire two weeks she was at the Tyler hospital with her husband. Each of the people incorrectly assumed that she had authorized the woodcutters to cut the wood. One of the wood thieves had even asked one of her neighbors who the landowner was and was told her name. The thieves were seen cutting wood in the rain at times, apparently to get out as much wood from the place as possible before the owner showed up to stop them. One neighbor had copied down the license number of one of the woodcutter's trucks.

The landowner and a neighbor went to inspect the area where the woodcutting had taken place. They found that the thieves had cut timber along the road for a full half mile on her land. One of her son-in-laws estimated that up to thirty cords of wood had been cut and hauled away.

So far this was one of those typical cases where someone living in or near a large city thinks that if they drive into the country about a hundred miles they can do almost anything they please with impunity from either the law or the local residents living there. This may be possible elsewhere, but it won't work in Leon County and it certainly won't work if they happen to pick this fiery-eyed southern lady's land on which to commit their crimes.

After discovering that the thieves had stolen far more wood than she had realized, she called Wood Thief Jr. using the telephone number he had given her. She advised him that she knew that he and his cohorts had been stealing wood for days while she was absent and threatened to bring charges against him for trespassing and theft. His reply was that if she would not press charges he would come back to Flo and work out a satisfactory solution to his problem with her. She agreed. When he arrived with his girlfriend and a couple of her children, she asked him how many cords of wood he and his friends had cut. He estimated that they had cut between eighteen and twenty cords.

"What do I have to do to satisfy you," he asked.

"Cut me eighteen cords of wood, each piece between eight and ten inches in diameter and bring it to my house and stack it. If that's not to your liking, you can pay me for eighteen cords, at the price you charge your customers." He decided he would rather bring her the wood.

On the following day of that same weekend, Wood Thief Jr. arrived with his father (referred to hereafter as Wood Thief Sr.). They cut wood for a while and brought it to her house in the truck. Some of the pieces were so large that she could barely lift them and they would not fit into the Franklin stove in her house. She measured one piece and found it to be nineteen and a half inches in diameter.

"Why lady," Wood Thief Sr. said to her after she complained to him about the logs' size and weight, "I'm sixty two years old and I can lift these logs." He was apparently trying to save face in front of his son.

"I'm sixty-four years old and I shouldn't be expected to lift them," she replied.

Her son-in-law, who happened to be there at the time, advised her that the larger pieces could be split only with a hydraulic log splitter. She told the thieves to load the big pieces back on their truck to take them to their home to split them and return them to her on a later trip.

She didn't see or hear from the thieves again for about a week. They still owed her about seventeen cords of wood. She called them again. They stated that they would come the next day but didn't show up. She called them again and gave them a deadline for completing their verbal contract to provide her the wood. Wood Thief Sr., along with another elderly man that was his helper, arrived at last but did not bring the wood they had hauled away earlier to split.

Her next difficulty with Wood Thief Sr. concerned the size of a cord of wood. When she measured the wood she found that what they were calling a "cord" was in reality about three-fourths of a cord. Wood Thief Sr. said, "Anyone should know that three rows of wood in the bed of a pickup that is level with the top of the pickup bed is a cord." What he apparently didn't realize was that he was not talking to a fool.

"Wouldn't you agree that the size of the truck bed has something to do with it? A cord of wood is four feet high, four feet wide, and eight feet long and your truck isn't that large."

It had by now turned into a daily hassle with the thieves to get them to cut wood and deliver it to her and stack it properly. They were still trying to dodge their responsibility at every opportunity. They even laid out an area for stacking a cord of wood that was only thirteen feet long instead of the required sixteen feet (the stack was only two feet wide and therefore had to be sixteen feet long). She was also having trouble getting them to come by her house on their way to cut wood so that she would know that it was them and not even more wood thieves cutting wood on her place.

In the January 31 issue of the *Dallas Morning News* the lady found the following classified ad under the "Wood,Fuel,Oil" section of the newspaper:

Seasoned Oak. $140.00 Cord. $75.00 1/2 Cord.

The ad also listed a telephone number. It was the same number that Wood Thief Jr. had given her when she caught him stealing her wood the day after she brought her husband home from the hospital.

One day the lady was away with her husband getting him a medical checkup when one of her neighbor's sons saw the thieves cutting wood on her land. Not knowing that they were authorized to be there cutting wood for her, he promptly went to them, took the keys out of their truck, and made what might be considered a citizen's arrest of Wood Thief Sr. He took him in his own vehicle to the landowner's house and, when he found her absent, took him to his own mother's house down the road a half mile away and ordered him inside. The thief complained of being a diabetic and asked if he could have a bite to eat. The mother promptly fed him a jelly sandwich which was the only thing she had to offer at the moment. She and her son were frantically trying to find the landowner by calling all the places they could think of that she and her husband might be. Finally, the son took Wood Thief Sr. back to where his helper was waiting for them. About this time, the landowner came by heading home with her husband. When she saw the thieves she wheeled her vehicle into the area where they were, jumped out, and berated them for not coming by her home each time they came to her place to let her know they were there to cut wood. She then whirled about to give another man a bad time and discovered that he was her neighbor's son trying to protect her property. "Hi, Arty, what are you doing here?" she asked, rather lamely.

"I caught them cutting your wood," he replied.

She looked over at her vehicle and saw that her husband was very upset. She left the area immediately and took him home where she called Arty's mother, who was also a nurse, and asked her to come over and take care of her husband while she returned to the fray with the thieves. She left the house and her husband before her neighbor arrived.

When she returned to the thieves, Arty asked her what she wanted to do, but recommended that she call the sheriff. She asked Wood Thief Sr., in Arty's presence, at what price he had been selling her wood. He agreed that they were asking $140.00 per cord. When she told him that he could pay that amount for each cord he still owed her, he objected, stating that she was asking too much. He wanted to subtract all his expenses for cutting, hauling, delivery and stacking the wood at his customers' location. In other words he wanted her to subsidize him for the stealing of her wood! She flatly refused the very idea.

Knowing the nature of law enforcement in Leon County, she decided to give him one last chance to cut and deliver her wood. He agreed to do so. Arty, after telling him that he had heard him make the commitment to fulfill his verbal contract, left the area.

About this time her nurse friend arrived in a near panic. "I can't find your husband," she cried. "He's nowhere in the house. He's disappeared!"

"He's got to be there," said the landowner (she had visions of him lying unconscious in the bathroom). "Go back and search the house!" Her nurse friend ran for the house again and discovered that the landowner's husband had gone for a walk down the road to their mailbox.

Eventually, the whole agreement fell apart when she discovered that the thieves would cut wood until midmorning, deliver it to her house then cut wood for a couple of hours before leaving for lunch. At lunch time on a couple of these days, she went to where they were cutting the wood and could find no wood. She concluded that they were stealing the wood at lunch time that they cut late in the morning. The same thing was happening in the afternoon; that is, they were taking wood home with them at night. She couldn't believe that they were so brazen that they continued to steal her wood while paying off a debt for wood they had stolen earlier!

The final confrontation occurred one day when she continued to object to Wood Thief Sr. continuing to deliver wood to her that was too large to use. By now he was also putting pieces of tree limbs and chunks of old rotted wood in to fill up space to make a cord.

"There is no more small wood where we are cutting along the road," he complained.

"That's the whole point," she said. "You've sold your customers all of the wood that is a proper size and now you're trying to deliver me unusable wood that is too large and otherwise unsatisfactory."

Wood Thief Sr. was now irate, not only at her but especially at Arty. He came around his truck toward her and with a raised voice said, "Arty wasn't even on his land. He was on your land. I'm going to file charges against him and if you support him I'm going to file charges against you!"

This lady felt like flattening him then and there but instead merely bowed to him and said, "Make my day!" She then ordered him to leave her property and never set foot on it again. She turned and headed for her house.

"That's right," he sang out to her in a sing-song voice like a ten-year old ridiculing another kid, "go in and call the law."

"I'm not calling the law. I'm going in for my shotgun," she replied.

Once inside her house she called the Leon County sheriff's office and a deputy was sent out. He stopped at her house and she told him where he could find the thieves. He went to where they were still cutting wood, talked to them and presumably recorded the license numbers from their vehicles. She arrived a short time later.

"We aren't thieves until you prove that we stole your wood," Wood Thief Sr. said to her.

"You're not only a thief but now you're a liar as well." For the benefit of the deputy she again ordered the thieves to leave and never return. She explained to the deputy about her husband's condition and how he had been affected by the stress of the series of confrontations she had with them. The deputy asked them to leave her property. As they prepared to go, she told the deputy that the wood they were about to leave with belonged to her so he had them unload it on the spot.

During the process of unloading the wood, Wood Thief Sr. asked the deputy, "Where do I go to file charges against her?"

"At the court in Centerville. That's where I'm going. Just follow me." This didn't please the lady at all for it sounded almost like an invitation to the thieves to file charges against her, although she was the county resident and they were the trespassing thieves. She got into her car to follow the thieves and the deputy to Centerville to file her own charges, but decided to do it later for her husband needed her at the moment.

At this writing she has not been notified that any charges were filed against either her or Arty. She realizes that the most convenient thing she could do would be to just forget the whole thing. She is not concerned about receiving pay for the stolen wood or in getting the fifteen cords of wood still owed her. What was violated was not only the law, but her principles as well. She is still seriously considering filing charges against the thieves for, at least, trespassing, theft, and reckless endangerment of her husband's life.

PHOTOGRAPHS

FROM

LEON COUNTY

1. The author at the Flo store, 1991

2. Evan Moore, storyteller.
   Story 19, 24, 30, 41, 44, 49, 51

3. The Flo croosroads church

4. Joe Bell, last of his kind. Story 4, 5, 47

5. Typical one-lane dirt road in Flo

6. Flying Jenny. Depression era merry-go-round

7. Wendel Bell. Accidentally shot by the sheriff.
   Story 50

8. Typical Flo home of the 1930's

9. The Grapevine Booby Trap. Story 10

10. "Old Town" Buffalo. Scene of Miller/Lenson gunfight. Story 13

ORDER FORM

Telephone Orders: Call (303) 794-7691

Postal Order: Wheelock Creek Publishing Company
6742 S. Downing Circle E.
Littleton, CO 80122

Please send the following book(s):

Quantity _____ <u>Book Title</u>

_____ <u>REFLECTIONS FROM THE FLO CROSSROADS</u>

Discounts: 1 book, $14.95, no discount
2-4 books, 10% discount, ($13.45 per book)
5-10 books, 20% discount, ($11.96 per book)

Sales Tax: Please add 57 cents for each book
shipped to Colorado addresses.

Shipping: $1.50 for the first book and 75 cents for each
additional book.

Payment: Check   Money Order

ORDER NOW
Wheelock Creek Publishing Company
6742 S. Downing Circle E.
Littleton, CO 80122